PRAISE FOR THE
Curious Encounters of the Human Kind
SERIES

"Most of Paul Sochaczewski's curious encounters start out as intelligent travel writing, exploring hidden corners of Asia and characters very much out of the ordinary. But this series works on a more complex level: he frequently zooms in and out of left field with a curious tangent, a sensitive reminiscence, a provocative opinion, a new way of looking at events that already are beyond most 'normal' travelers' tales. I read each story feeling refreshed, enlightened, and curious to see what the next stage of Sochaczewski's journey would bring."

—JUDITH M. HEIMANN, author of *The Most Offending Soul Alive: Tom Harrisson and His Remarkable Life* and *The Airmen and the Headhunters: A True Story of Lost Soldiers, Heroic Tribesmen and the Unlikeliest Rescue of World War II*

"What a discovery! Paul Sochaczewski is that rarest of writers who knows that the real 'Asian miracle' isn't malls or computer geeks. In his years traveling the continent, he has discovered an eternal assemblage of arcane explorers, putative emperors, frivolous mystics, sacrosanct elephants and, yes, miracle workers. When Sochaczewski finds them, in Javanese palaces or sacred forests protected by spirits, they are caviar (or sweetened bird's nest) for his fascinating portraits. This series is for everyone who knows that the Mysterious East is alive and well, and more how-about-that-wonderful than you perhaps imagined."

—HARRY ROLNICK, author of *The Chinese Gourmet, The Complete Book of Coffee,* and *Spice Chronicles: Exotic Tales of a Hungry Traveler*

"Paul Sochaczewski skips about Asia like a Monkey God hopping from mountain to mountain, bringing back life-prolonging peaches while annoying the gatekeepers. Whatever you do, follow him on this journey!"

—LEE CHOR LIN, director of the National Museum of Singapore; former curator of Asian Civilizations Museum – Singapore; author of *Batik: Creating an Identity*

"Sochaczewski is a world-class searcher, reporter, and observer who has criss-crossed Asia for forty years, pausing in the most unlikely places and finding extraordinary people. The essays in these insightful and witty chronicles present a rich tapestry of eccentric nobles, self-serving naturalists, scoundrels who will make your teeth ache, celebrity monks, and memorable folks whose stories are too good to be true. But they are."

—CHRISTOPHER G. MOORE, author of the Vincent Calvino novels and *Heart Talk*

"In this series Sochaczewski explores the hidden corners, the forgotten people, and their surprising tales. All the personal traveler's tales in these volumes are captivating, all filled with humor, drama, and insight, with an edgy take-no-prisoners voice. You won't find anything else like this on the bookshelf."

—JEFF MCNEELY, chief scientist, International Union for Conservation of Nature

"The *Curious Encounters of the Human Kind* series is a delicious stew of improbable characters and intriguing stories, served up in thoroughly pithy style, and with a hearty dash of irreverent humour."

—TIM HANNIGAN, author of *Raffles and the British Invasion of Java* and *Brief History of Indonesia: Sultans, Spices, and Tsunamis: The Incredible Story of Southeast Asia's Largest Nation*

"Constructed on a base of strange but true personal travel adventures, *Curious Encounters* adds elements of history, an edgy sense of humour, mysticism, political incorrectness, current affairs, and memorable characters you'll wish you had the pleasure to meet on your travels. Consider each book in this series like a good curry – the result is more than the sum of its parts; each tale has its own zing. Travel with these books to the little-visited corners of Asia, and savour them.

—JASON BROOKE, director of The Brooke Trust

"I never tire of living vicariously through Paul Sochaczewski and his writing adventures. He keeps finding these wonderful details that miraculously open up entire worlds to be explored. Paul is the last of the Great Hunters, only instead of trophies, it is stories he brings home for our admiration, wonder, and delight."

—MARK OLSHAKER, Emmy-winning filmmaker; author of *Einstein's Brain*, *The Edge*, and *Mindhunter*

"The *Curious Encounters* series is proof positive that a writer/traveler can immerse himself in Asian cultures and yet remain objective enough to write extremely entertaining and often irreverent articles and colorful stories about what he has experienced. From Indonesian mystics to Burmese white elephant hunters, the descriptions are spot-on. There is something in these articles and stories that reminds me of the writing of Paul Theroux – not as cynical, perhaps, but the author is just as able to look at events with a clear, unsentimental and yet sympathetic eye. You won't regret a moment spent reading these tales, which perfectly capture the allure and spice of the places visited."

—DEAN BARRETT, author of *Memoirs of a Bangkok Warrior*

VOLUMES IN THE
Curious Encounters of the Human Kind
SERIES:

Myanmar (Burma)

Indonesia

Himalaya: India, Bhutan, Nepal

Borneo

Southeast Asia:
Thailand, Laos, Cambodia, Vietnam, the Philippines

OTHER TITLES BY PAUL SOCHACZEWSKI

Share Your Journey

An Inordinate Fondness for Beetles

The Sultan and the Mermaid Queen

Redheads

Distant Greens

Eco-Bluff Your Way to Greenism

Soul of the Tiger

CURIOUS
ENCOUNTERS
of the
HUMAN KIND

BORNEO

CURIOUS
ENCOUNTERS
of the
HUMAN KIND

BORNEO

True Asian Tales of
Folly, Greed, Ambition
and Dreams

PAUL SPENCER SOCHACZEWSKI

EXPLORER'S EYE PRESS

GENEVA, SWITZERLAND

Cover photo: A young girl looks after her sister at an isolated Kayan longhouse in Sarawak.

All photos by Paul Sochaczewski, except where noted.

Jeffrey A. McNeely contributed to an earlier version of "The Literate Orangutan." David J.S. Hallmark contributed to an earlier version of "Pass Me a Rat, I'm a Survivor."

ISBN: 978-2-940573-10-3

Published by:
Explorer's Eye Press
Geneva, Switzerland

Book design by Stacey Aaronson
Map of Borneo by John Welding

Printed in the United States of America

Dedicated to the people of Asia who shared their stories,
and sometimes their homes, rice wine, termite omelets,
and dreams.

TABLE OF CONTENTS

Author's Note

AUTHOR'S NOTE

Some thoughts about change in Borneo:

Borneo (made up of the Malaysian states of Sabah and Sarawak, the Indonesian provinces of West, South, Central, East, and North Kalimantan, and the Sultanate of Brunei) has changed dramatically in some ways during the last few decades.

Some of the change is positive – certainly there are improvements in health care, education, and communications (depending on their remoteness, most settled communities have television and cell phones).

The cities vary from charming to functional; all urban areas in Borneo have sophisticated services, good air transport, universities, hospitals, banks, and, that most important element of Asian sophistication, vast air-conditioned shopping malls.

Transport, which once in the interior was restricted to river traffic, has been made considerably easier by main trunk roads and air routes connecting major cities (except for Kalimantan, where a trip from, say, Pontianak to Banjarmasin is impossible by road and requires a flight to Jakarta and then a second flight to the destination). Interior communities also have better access to roads, but these are largely a byproduct of extensive timber operations and oil palm plantations. Such roads come at a heavy cost. Virtually all of Sarawak, Sabah, and Kalimantan have been home to a painful and unceasing stew of rampant deforestation, abuse of native land rights, and brown-

brown colonialism. Only Brunei, among the richest countries in the world, has protected its rainforest to a significant extent.

When I was first writing this book, it was heavy with stories about kleptocracy, unforgivable crimes against human rights and nature, dead orangutans, and shattered dreams.

But I've sought out feel-good stories as well, and I hope I have been able to present the basic goodness of the people accurately. Take away the corrupt government leaders, the voracious timber merchants, the insatiable oil palm plantation owners, and you've got a pretty wonderful place. (For a satiric fictional view of schizophrenic orangutans, self-serving government officials, fraudulent scientists, inept western conservationists, and sexy researchers, you might be interested in my novel *Redheads*.)

Some of these chapters were written, in simpler forms, over a period of several decades. While in some cases statistics might have changed in recent years, the basic truth of the human stories offered here of foibles, ambitions, and achievements remains constant.

You can write, I know you can.

Photo: Jeffrey A. McNeely

THE LITERATE ORANGUTAN

We share 96.4% of our DNA with orangutans –
is that enough to call them family?

SEPILOK, SABAH, MALAYSIA

hat if we could communicate with other species?
What could an orangutan tell us about her life, about her emotions when her rainforest is chopped down, about the rascally behavior of randy adolescent male orangutans?

I'VE SEEN ORANGUTANS IN THE WILD, AN INCREASINGLY rare occurrence since the big red apes are scarce and becoming even more difficult to spot. They can be touchy; if they feel threatened they might pelt you with branches.

But for pure pleasure it's hard to beat a one-on-one encounter with a rehabilitant orangutan.

I was sitting under a tree at the Sepilok Nature Reserve, in Sabah, Malaysia, when a seven-year-old orangutan named BJ wandered over. He was a "rehabilitant," an unfortunate word that describes the dozens of apes at Sepilok that had been captured for the illegal pet trade and then confiscated by Malaysian officials. I looked into BJ's eyes and was reminded of a comment made by Malcolm MacDonald, former governor-general of colonial Malaya and Borneo:

> These members of the order Primates contemplate you, when you meet them, with melancholy eyes, as if they had just read Darwin's *Origin of Species* and were painfully aware of being your poor relations who have not done so well in life.

They certainly *look* smart, and we *want* them to be smart, but really, how intelligent are they?

Shuffling upright, with his red arms hanging almost to his ankles, BJ hunkered down, leaned over my shoulder, and watched me scribble notes.

"I can teach you to write, BJ," I optimistically said, half expecting him to respond. I engaged BJ in a deep, meaningful stare. "This is how you write your name." I wrote the initials BJ and said the letters. "BEE-JAY." BJ's chin was on my shoulder. Before I could repeat the exercise, BJ ripped the notebook out of my hands, stuck it in his mouth, and scampered up a tree.

BJ returned and I had a tug of war with him over my school exercise book, now minus a cover, which lodged in the ape's stomach. I don't think this was literary criticism, and I should have been grateful that BJ's energies took such benign form, since wild male orangutans have been known to attack people. BJ, however, having been raised by people and treated as a surrogate son, had had much of the wildness taken from him, and when I scolded him he eventually relinquished the notebook. I was the alpha male, the orangutan equivalent of the big orangutan patriarch with the cheek pouches, parallel to the gorilla silverback. BJ took his place again at my side, as docile as a golden retriever, his chin leaning on my shoulder, his arm casually draped around my neck. He reached for the pen. Ah, I thought. Good lad. He's going to try to write. Instead, BJ chewed the Bic like a candy cane. I snatched it back and dried the pen on his red hair. He matched my action by grabbing a twig and rubbing it on my salt and pepper chest hair.

This orangutan wasn't making my ape-human break-through very easy. Eventually BJ settled down and I continued writing for the third time. "Watch me: BEE – JAY. BEE – JAY." I looked into his eyes. He looked at me. We had made contact. I had a protégé. "BEE – JAY. BEE – JAY. BEE ..." Faster than the downstroke of the J, BJ had nipped off the button on the epaulet of my quick-dry, look-like-a-real-explorer jungle shirt and darted up a nearby tree, all the while making soft whistling noises through the button.

BJ'S RELATIVES ARE BEING SHOT IN A SIMILAR MANNER TO the way they were killed during the mid-nineteenth century, when Victorian naturalist Alfred Russel Wallace famously shot, skinned, boiled, and pickled seventeen of the red apes.

Wallace recalled how the hunt evolved:

> Some Dyaks [sic] saw another mias [local name for orangutan] … and came to tell me. We found it to be a rather large one, very high up on a tall tree. At the second shot it fell, rolling over, but almost immediately got up again and began to climb. At a third shot it fell dead. This was also a full-grown female, and while preparing to carry it home, we found a young one face downward in the bog. This little creature was only about a foot long, and had evidently been hanging to its mother when she first fell. Luckily it did not appear to have been wounded, and after we had cleaned the mud out of its mouth it began to cry out, and seemed quite strong and active.

Wallace grew attached to the baby ape, soppily writing:

> I must tell you of the addition to my household of an orphan baby ... which I have nursed now more than a month ... I am afraid you would call it an ugly baby, for it has dark brown skin and red hair, very large mouth ... It has powerful lungs, and sometimes screams tremendously, so I hope it will live. Don't be alarmed; I was the cause of its mother's death ... I can safely say, what so many have said before with much less truth, 'There never was such a baby as my baby,' and I am sure nobody ever had such a dear little duck of a darling of a little brown hairy baby before.

MOST PEOPLE WHO WORK WITH ORANGUTANS HAVE made emotional connections with the apes.

Biruté Galdikas, who has spent four decades living with orangutans at Tanjung Puting, in Kalimantan, Indonesian Borneo, tells of how one of her "rehabilitant" charges named Sugito reacted to human mothering. In doing so she also provided insight on how the human-ape contact brought out her own mothering instincts.

"I had raised Sugito from infancy," Biruté Galdikas recalled in a 1980 issue of *National Geographic*. "I had cuddled him, called him endearing names, and handed him tidbits of food. Taking my cue from the wild orangutan mothers I was observing, I had let him cling to me night and day."

Alfred Russel Wallace too was "mothering." Seldom has he written passages of such tenderness and humor than those he penned about his "little brown hairy baby" while in Sarawak.

> When handled or nursed, [the baby orangutan] was very quiet and contented, but when laid down by itself would invariably cry; and for the first few nights was very restless and noisy. I fitted up a little box for a cradle, with a soft mat for it to lie upon, which was changed and washed every day, and I soon found it necessary to wash the little mias as well. After I had done so a few times, it came to like the operation, and as soon as it was dirty would begin crying, and not leave off till I took it out and carried it to the spout,

when it immediately became quiet, although it would wince a little at the first rush of the cold water and make ridiculously wry faces while the stream was running over its head. It enjoyed the wiping and rubbing dry amazingly, and when I brushed its hair seemed to be perfectly happy, lying quite still, with its arms and legs stretched out ... For the first few days it clung desperately with all four hands to whatever it could lay hold of, and I had to be careful to keep my beard out of its way, as its fingers clutched hold of hair more tenaciously than anything else, and it was impossible to free myself without assistance ... I endeavored to make an artificial mother, by wrapping up a piece of buffalo-skin into a bundle, and suspending it about a foot from the floor. At first this seemed to suit it admirably ... I was now in hopes that I had made the little orphan quite happy; and so it seemed for some time till it began to remember its lost parent and try to suck. It would pull itself up close to the skin, and try about everywhere for a likely place; but, as it only succeeded in getting mouthfuls of hair and wool, it would be greatly disgusted, and scream violently, and, after two or three attempts, let go altogether. One day it got some wool into its throat, and I thought it would have choked, but after much gasping it recovered, and I was obliged to take the imitation mother to pieces again.

Wallace noted how helpless the orangutan infant was compared to a monkey of similar age.

After I had had the little mias about three weeks, I fortunately obtained a young hare-lip monkey (Macacus cynomolgus), which, though small, was very active, and could feed itself. I placed it in the same box with the mias, and they immediately became excellent friends. The little monkey would sit upon the other's stomach, or even on its face, without the least regard to its feelings ... and as soon as I had finished would pick off what was left sticking to the mias's lips, and then pull open its mouth and see if any still remained inside. The little helpless mias would submit to all these insults with the most exemplary patience, only too glad to have something warm near it.

It was curious to observe the different actions of these two animals, which could not have differed much in age. The mias, like every young baby, lying on its back quite helpless, rolling lazily from side to side, wishing to grasp something, but hardly able to guide its fingers to any definite object and expressing its wants by a most infantine scream; the little monkey, on the other hand, in constant motion, seizing hold of the smallest objects with the greatest precision.

But no amount of loving can replace basic nutrition.

After five weeks [the mias] cut its two upper front teeth, but in all this time it had not grown the least bit ... no doubt owing to the want of milk [it suffered] an attack of diarrhoea ... but a small dose of castor-oil ... cured it. A week or two afterward it was again taken ill, and this time more seriously. The symptoms were exactly those of intermittent fever, accompanied by watery swellings on the feet and head ... after lingering for a week a most pitiable object, died, after being in my possession nearly three months. I much regretted the loss of my little pet, which I had at one time looked forward to bringing up to years of maturity, and taking home to England.

Wallace's tender touch only went so far – when the "little duck of a darling" died, Wallace unceremoniously skinned it and boiled the bones in a giant iron skillet for sale to a British museum.

> Its weight was three pounds nine ounces, its height fourteen inches, and the spread of its arms twenty-three inches. I preserved its skin and skeleton, and in doing so found that when it fell from the tree it must have broken an arm and a leg, which had, however, united so rapidly that I had only noticed the hard swellings on the limbs where the irregular junction of the bones had taken place.

JUST AS WALLACE LET HIS MIAS "CHILD" PLAY WITH THE monkey, Biruté Galdikas in Kalimantan also encouraged cross-species fraternizing among her biological son Bin-Bin and the rehabilitant orangutans at the isolated camp in the swamp forest. Having few human children to play with, Bin-Bin naturally made friends with the juvenile red apes. One particular playmate was Princess, a young orangutan that researcher Gary Shapiro was trying to teach to speak American Sign Language. Bin-Bin-the-boy and Princess-the-orangutan communicated in basic sign language, which probably included gestures of their own creation. Unfortunately Bin-Bin's human contacts were less fruitful, and when I met the tyke I said "hello" in English and got no response. "Hello" in Indonesian brought a glimmer of recognition. "Hello" in hooting

Gibbon brought squeals of delight. Ultimately, Bin-Bin's father Rod Brindamour decided that California might be a better place for his son than a sticky black-river campsite overrun by spoiled red apes, and father and son moved to the States.

Sugito, Biruté Galdikas's surrogate orangutan-child, who was allowed to run free while her biological son Bin-Bin was sometimes kept caged for his own protection, developed human-like psychoses. "Now Sugito was 7," Galdikas wrote, "and I faced the dreadful consequences of inadvertently raising an orangutan as a human being – an adolescent who was not only incredibly curious, active, and tool using, but one who killed." For despite Biruté Galdikas's best mothering efforts, Sugito had picked up a bad habit – he held baby orangutans under the water until they drowned. Even more troubling, Sugito had tried the same trick with a human visitor to the research camp.

Galdikas, like any mother with a child turned criminal, was puzzled and distraught, since wild orangutans are normally not killers. "Sugito was something different," she rationalized. "Perhaps the biblical analogy was apt: Raised by a human mother and exposed to human culture, he had eaten of the 'tree of knowledge' and lost his orangutan innocence. Now, in a very non-orangutan way, he was acting out his jealousy of the infants who had seemingly replaced him in my affection."

WHEN WALLACE WENT TO SOUTHEAST ASIA, PEOPLE were not sure whether the orangutan was a big monkey or a lower form of human being. Wallace pondered the differences between people and other animals; he asked whether orangutans have egos and if so what would be the evolutionary benefit of such a gift.

> If man is but a highly intellectual animal developed from a lower animal form under the law of the survival of the fittest, how did this "second-self," this "unconscious ego," come into existence? Have the mollusk and the reptile, the dog and the ape, "unconscious egos"? And if so, why? And what use are they to these creatures, so that they might have been developed by means of the struggle for existence?

The question of whether other forms of life have consciousness has challenged philosophers and scientists for millennia. And the orangutan, because of its similarities to a human in so many ways, has always been a particularly provocative companion.

The first westerner to describe the orangutan was Dutchman Jacob de Bondt (Bontius). In the early seventeenth century, he presented a drawing of a female who:

> hid her secret parts with no great modesty from unknown men, and also her face with her hands (if one may speak thus), weeping copiously, uttering groans, and expressing other human acts so that you would say nothing human was lacking in her but speech. The Javanese say, in truth, that they can talk, but do not

wish to, lest they should be compelled to labor. The name they give to it is Ourang Outang, which means a man of the woods, and they affirm that they are born from the lust of the Indian women, who mix with apes and monkeys with detestable sensuality.

Wallace used the scientific name *Simia satyrus* (which roughly means the pathologically active sexual ape) to describe the orangutan; it was only decades later that scientists re-classified the orangutan, whose Malay/Indonesian name means "person of the forest," as *Pongo pygmaeus* for the two Borneo varieties and *Pongo abelii* for the Sumatran variety.

The *satyrus* appellation is accurate, though, since orangutans certainly are sexual.

At Biruté Galdikas's Camp Leakey in Kalimantan, which includes an orangutan rehabilitation station, schizophrenic orangutans jump the animal/human line all the time. They murder. They rape. They steal. They vandalize. They refuse to pay attention in class. They put dirty things in their mouths. They beg. They act like people.

Male orangutans have been known to sexually assault women. Syarif Kassim Alkadrie, the second Sultan of Pontianak in southern Borneo, who ruled from 1808 to 1819, told J. Burn, an English visitor, that an orangutan had carried off one of his female slaves. The animal kept the woman prisoner for some fourteen months, but she later escaped. When the Sultan sensed that Burn was skeptical, Burn replied that he believed the story, since he had heard from others that such kidnappings were common in the region. And a story with better credibility: Galdikas tells of how Gondul, a rehabilitant orangutan she had raised from infancy (for a while Gondul slept with Biruté Galdikas and her husband Rod Brindamour), grabbed the cook, ripped off her sarong, and tried to rape her.

YOUNG WILD MALE ORANGUTANS JUST ENTERING adulthood are often rapists. The females normally enjoy voluntary sex only with the large dominant males. These mighty animals, whose huge throat sacs, long hair, and wide cheek flanges are badges of their fully mature masculinity, are capable of defending a territory against other males seeking mates. The young males, who are fully mature sexually yet are not powerful enough to establish a territory of their own, skulk around the forest quietly by themselves trying to avoid the dominant males. Even a barely mature male orangutan is much larger than a fully adult female, so when he comes across a female, rape often ensues. Perhaps Gondul had experienced an identity crisis from his long years in captivity and was not quite clear on the distinction between people and orangutans. The boundaries were blurred. If rape was normal for him, why not rape a female human?

FOR A CINEMATOGRAPHIC PARALLEL, ONE MIGHT LOOK at the closing sequence in the 1981 film *Tarzan the Ape Man* (featuring an orangutan found only in Malaysia and

Indonesia in a movie allegedly set in Africa but shot in Sri Lanka), in which actress Bo Derek came dangerously close to being sexually assaulted by the orangutan. Miles O'Keeffe, her leading man, was tossed aside by the enamored, seemingly tame, ape. *Playboy* magazine, in a picture spread showing the incident, noted that during a love scene:

> C.J., the jealous orangutan, didn't much like the idea of Tarzan and Jane having fun without him. In a totally impromptu move, he pulled 195-pound Miles O'Keeffe off Bo, interrupting one of the movie's steamier scenes ... "We wrestled with him for an hour and a half," recalled Derek. "Orangutans are several times stronger than people and have four things to grab you with."

JUST AS MALE ORANGUTANS CAN BE AS AGGRESSIVE AS men, female orangutans can be victimized like women. John MacKinnon, one of the few scientists who has studied all three of the great apes in the wild, reported that several Dayak longhouses in central Kalimantan keep female orangutans in the longhouse for use as primate equivalents of inflatable dolls. In an article in the British journal *New Scientist*, he called the world's attention to the danger that Dayak men, tempted by a long evening's revelry, might spread venereal disease through at least part of the wild orangutan population by infecting captive female orangutans that are later released in the wild.

CONSERVATION SCIENTIST MICHAEL KAVANAGH alerted the world to the fact that female orangutans seldom get pregnant from rape, which happens rather frequently, but readily get pregnant from mutually agreed sex. One reason, according to Kavanagh: female orangutans only experience orgasm during mutually pleasurable sex, rarely during rape, and the contractions of the female's uterus during orgasm suck the semen in the direction of the egg that is waiting to be fertilized.

CARL LINNAEUS, THE SWEDISH SCIENTIST WHO developed the modern scheme of binomial nomenclature, the system used for modern taxonomy, said: "It is remarkable that the stupidest ape differs so little from the wisest man, that the surveyor of nature has yet to be found who can draw the line between them."

Sue Savage-Rumbaugh, who has studied the intelligence of a number of ape species, argues that the orangutans's human-like emotions, intellect, and ability to acquire language should make them eligible for "semi-human" legal status. She is convinced that orangutans are at least "morally equivalent" to profoundly mentally challenged children. "We certainly would not put these children in a zoo to be gawked at as examples of nature," she says, "nor would we permit medical experimentation to be conducted on them."

In 2014 the association of lawyers for animal rights in Argentina, ALFADA, submitted a habeas corpus petition on behalf of Sandra, a twenty-nine-year-old Sumatran orangutan that had spent the previous twenty years in captivity at the Buenos Aires (Argentina) zoo. The appeal cited "the unjustified confinement of an animal with probable cognitive capability." The lawyers requested that an orangutan should be considered a "non-human person" with some of the same legal rights as a human; she should not be treated as an object. They requested that she be transferred to a less confining primate sanctuary in Brazil.

Leif Cocks, who has some twenty-five years of experience in rescuing and rehabilitating captive orangutans, and Gary Shapiro, the man who tried to teach Princess American Sign Language, supported Sandra's case, arguing:

> In a being [such as an orangutan] with a high level of consciousness and sensibility, loss of freedom and loss of choice to a high degree is a form of suffering ... Sandra is a unique ape person with her own history, character and preferences that need to be respected in making a decision that suits her.

As of September 2015, Sandra's case is still being considered by the Argentine courts.

ALFRED RUSSEL WALLACE AND CHARLES DARWIN agreed on many things but disagreed on one major point: They strongly differed about whether natural selection applied to people.

Charles Darwin felt that *Homo sapiens* was simply a product of the same process of natural selection that applies to all other creatures, and that "Man still bears in his bodily frame the indelible stamp of his lowly origins."

But Alfred Russel Wallace felt that the mechanism of natural selection alone accounted for everything up to, but *not* including, *Homo sapiens*. Reviewing Darwin's theory, Wallace wrote:

> [Darwin concluded that] Man's whole nature – physical, mental, intellectual, and moral – was developed from the lower animals by means of the same laws of variation and survival; and, as a consequence of this belief ... there was no difference in kind between man's nature and animal nature, but only one of degree.

Wallace thought there *was* a difference in kind, and asked why some skills, seemingly not essential to survival, developed:

> [This class of human faculties] cannot, therefore, be thus accounted for. Such are the capacity to form ideal conceptions of space and time, of eternity, and infinity – the capacity for intense artistic feelings of pleasure – and for those abstract notions ... which render geometry and arithmetic possible ... How were all or any of these faculties first developed, when they could have been of no possible use to man in his early stages of barbarism? How could "natural selection", or survival of the fittest in the struggle for existence, at all favor the development of mental powers so entirely

removed from the material necessities of savage men ... The highly developed artistic and moral qualities of modern man could not be put down to natural selection.

How did such artistic, moral, and physical characteristics come about? Wallace, who was resolutely areligious, avoided using the word "God," but spoke of God-like forces:

Neither natural selection nor the more general theory of evolution can give any account whatever of the origin of sensational or conscious life. They may teach us how, by chemical, electrical, or higher natural laws, the organized body can be built up, can grow, can reproduce its like; but those laws and that growth cannot even be conceived as endowing the newly arranged atoms with consciousness. But the moral and higher intellectual nature of man is as unique a phenomenon as was conscious life on its first appearance in the world, and the one is almost as difficult to conceive as originating by any law of evolution as the other. We may even go further, and maintain that there are certain purely physical characteristics of the human race which are not explicable on the theory of variation and survival of the fittest. The brain, the organs of speech, the hand, and the external form of man, offer some special difficulties in this respect.

AND THE DEBATE GOES ON. HOW CLOSELY RELATED, physiologically and, more importantly, intellectually, are we with the orangutans of Borneo?

ARE ORANGUTANS SMART ENOUGH TO HAVE A conversation with?

While riding in a pram at Biruté Galdikas's spartan but functional base camp in Tanjung Puting, Princess, the five-year-old rehabilitant orangutan who was the pal of Galdikas's young son Bin-Bin, molded her hands into signs that meant: "You-Out-Up," indicating that she wanted to get out of that contraption and back on Papa's shoulder where she belonged. Swinging on one of her long arms, she hoisted herself onto Gary Shapiro's neck, her russet hair a close match for the American scientist's scraggly red beard.

While Princess tugged at his little remaining hair, Shapiro calmly explained what he was doing in the forest.

"I'm trying to teach Princess to speak Ameslan," Shapiro said. "That's American Sign Language, but I don't call it that since the Indonesian authorities might get up-tight about their orangutans learning a foreign language."

Galdikas considered Shapiro an important part of her research program. "My hope was that perhaps we could actually get into the orangutan's head," Galdikas explained, "and find out what she thinks about life in the forest, how she patterns her world."

School for Princess began at 06.45 in the morning. Shapiro sat her down squarely in front of a small table on which he placed a hand mirror. "Princess, *apa ini?*" he asked in spoken Indonesian, pointing to the mirror. What is this?

With all the excitement of a ten-year-old boy forced

to practice the piano when he'd rather be out playing football, Princess flicked her thumbnail against her teeth – the sign for "nut," which meant she thought she deserved a reward.

"Princess!" Shapiro yelled. "NO!"

Nevertheless, Shapiro gave Princess a peanut for her incorrect response, then patiently molded the correct response for "mirror" in which the signer shakes the flat hand repeatedly in front of the body, and took careful notes that he said would later be analyzed with the help of his university's computer.

He then replaced the mirror with a watch. Princess decided that Shapiro's pipe looked more interesting, and she grabbed it from the side table and started chewing. Shapiro was not amused since this was his last pipe – his student had already mangled two other briars.

"Apa ini?"

By this time Princess was standing on her head. She softly rolled over, scratched her belly, and started investigating my backpack, which was sitting in a corner of the wooden cabin.

"PRINCESS! You're gonna get it!"

I thought it was a novel pedagogical technique. Asking questions in Indonesian but scolding in English. And rewarding incorrect answers.

This time she got it right, touching her ear with her index finger. After her reward of two peanuts, she grabbed a woven bag and placed it over her head. She sat quietly, munching on an empty plastic film container.

The attempt to communicate was exasperating work, and as much as Shapiro and Princess obviously enjoyed being together – Galdikas claimed Shapiro was "an equal among equals" – the difficulty of teaching an ape who didn't want to be taught could have driven a lesser man to distraction.

EVEN FROM FIFTY METERS AWAY I COULD TELL THE orangutan sitting near the top of the rainforest tree in the Batang Air National Park in Sarawak was an adult male – his size, for one thing, as tall as a child but with the bulk of a rugby prop on steroids. Even more striking were his enlarged cheek pads and throat pouch, hairless hunks of flesh that framed his face into a silly grin. I quietly approached, but the big ape saw me coming and hurled dead branches at me, wanting to be left alone.

Some scientists say that soon an in-the-wild sighting like this will be impossible. Although some fifty to sixty thousand orangutans survive on the islands of Sumatra and Borneo, habitat loss, illegal logging, fires, and poaching are taking their toll. Willie Smits, head of the Borneo Orangutan Survival Foundation, predicts that if current trends continue, "in 20 years there will be no orangutans left in the wild."

No orangutans. No orangutan tales. Just the memory of a poor relative who hasn't done so well in life.

OVERPOPULATION OF
REHABILITANT ORANGUTANS

Biruté Galdikas's efforts have been so successful
(or Indonesian efforts to conserve rain forests have
been so pitiful) that Camp Leakey in Indonesia's
Tanjung Putting National Park has become home
to some six thousand rescued orangutans, far more
than the area can accommodate. Galdikas, whom
Reuters reported has some three hundred additional rescued orangutans in her care waiting to
join the animals at Camp Leakey, is trying to buy a
large plot of land opposite Tanjung Putting
National Park to accommodate the extra apes –
price tag $2.5 million.

Throw a party for young men coming of age.

WHY TRAVEL FAR?

The rite of passage and the teenage imperative.

BATANG AI, SARAWAK, MALAYSIA

I stood on a ridge near the border between Malaysian Sarawak and Indonesian Kalimantan. I had been gone half the day and had not brought food. Time to return to camp, a damp grouping of leaky impromptu shelters made out of saplings, leaves, and a few scraps of plastic fashioned by Iban tribesmen who obliged me in my desire to sleep rough. I knew where I was and was confident I could retrace my steps. But then I got ambitious. "What happens if I go down there instead?" I asked myself, heading toward a steep, trackless hill that my instincts told me would eventually connect to a tributary of my campsite river.

So I scampered, glided, bounced, scrunched, and thoroughly dirtied myself down the side of the mountain, finally reaching a meter-wide stream and a series of ridiculously pretty, pristine small waterfalls, which I slid down, with otter-like joy, but without otter-like grace. Chasing waterfalls. I was making no contribution to humanity in doing so, but I was fulfilling one of *my* basic needs – to get away from the crowd and do something modestly dangerous.

WHY TRAVEL FAR (AND TREACHEROUSLY), LEAVING behind comfort, friends, and security?

Peter Kedit, former director of the Sarawak Museum, feels my Asia travels are comparable to the concept of *berjalai* among the Iban tribe, the rite of passage for young men that in previous generations sometimes ended with the taking of a human head.

My mini-adventures are less bloody but serve a similar purpose. By leaving home and going off to the distant corners of the world, I have put down a marker. I am suggesting that when I return, *I will have been changed*. It is a desire to move toward individualization. *He* left and did exciting things that our left-behind friends can only dream about; *they* stayed and worked in the post office. Think of Kipling: "All things considered there are only two kinds of men in the world – those that stay at home and those that do not."

Neuroendocrinologist Robert Sapolsky discussed voluntary exile and adventure-seeking in the context of young male primates leaving the nest. "Another key to our success must have something to do with this voluntary transfer process, this primate legacy of getting an itch around adolescence," he wrote:

How did voluntary dispersal evolve? What is going on with that individual's genes, hormones, and neurotransmitters to make it hit the road? We don't know, but we do know that following this urge is one of the most resonantly primate of acts. A young male baboon stands riveted at the river's edge; an adolescent female chimp cranes to catch a glimpse of the chimps from the next valley. New animals, a whole bunch of 'em! To hell with logic and sensible behavior, to hell with tradition and respecting your elders, to hell with this drab little town, and to hell with that knot of fear in your stomach. Curiosity, excitement, adventure – the hunger for novelty is something fundamentally daft, rash, and enriching that we share with our whole taxonomic order.

COUCH POTATOES WHO NEVERTHELESS WANT TO experience some form of individuation might turn to collecting.

People collect matchbooks, stamps, and Elvis memorabilia. They collect numbers on locomotives and first-edition books. They collect rare Greek vases and beer mats and countless other things. Perhaps collecting exotic artifacts is sublimation for physical adventuring?

As a boy I collected rocks – I preferred the showy quartz varieties. I collected insects. I collected baseball cards and comic books. None of this is exceptional. Of all those collections, the only thing that has remained is my collection of ancient Roman coins. I was a bit of a nerd – the first article I ever published, at age fifteen, was about

Roman *denari*. Imagine, I thought, somebody two thousand years ago used this coin to buy lunch, or rent a donkey, or pay off a bet.

Collecting gets interesting, at least from the psychological angle, when it becomes obsessive, when a person's entire life is taken over by, say *Star Wars* toys or golf balls with logos of famous courses.

Sigmund Freud, himself an avid and sophisticated collector of classical, Egyptian, oriental, near-Eastern, and South American antiquities, suggested that collecting with great intensity was an outlet for a frustrated libido.

Freud recognized that collecting couldn't be dismissed easily. "The psychoanalyst, like the archaeologist, must uncover layer after layer of the patient's psyche, before coming to the deepest, most valuable treasures," he wrote.

Janine Burke, author of *The Gods of Freud: Sigmund Freud's Art Collection*, observes that a person's collection can reveal hidden personality traits. "The popular image of Freud as austere, remote and forbidding is contradicted by the collection," she wrote, "which reveals a very different personality: an impulsive, hedonistic spender, an informed and finicky aesthete, a tomb raider complicit in the often illegal trade in antiquities, a tourist who revelled in sensual, Mediterranean journeys, a generous fellow who lavished exquisite gifts on his family and friends, and a tough negotiator for a bargain. [Freud's] own therapy was shopping. Arranging choice items on his desk, Freud confessed to Carl Gustav Jung, 'I must always have an object to love.'"

SOCIETY FORGOT TO STAGE A CEREMONY JUST FOR ME. I came of age without a party. I was denied the vigil in the desert, where I was expected to kill a lion, fast for three weeks, have a vision, return to the village to get tattooed, become cleansed in a sweat lodge and decorated with feathers and body paint and invited, finally, to eat with the grown-ups.

We modern boys and girls lack rites of passage, rituals and ceremonies where we clearly shift from childhood to adulthood. Instead our life passages, at least in the developed West, are fuzzy. A confirmation or bar/bat mitzvah are important symbolically but take place before the participants are physically or emotionally adult. Girls in Western societies begin to menstruate many years before they are old enough to bear children in a socially acceptable context. Boys might be old enough to drive but not old enough to drink, old enough to kill/be killed in the army but not old enough to vote, old enough to father children but not old enough to leave school of their own volition.

If society doesn't offer us clear rites of passage, we tend to create our own.

Some boys will go into the army.

Some boys play competitive sports.

Some boys join gangs, or fraternities.

Some boys break into their fathers' gun cases and commit mayhem.

Some boys write novels, or sing on stage, or get a real job.

Some boys don't worry about it.

Some boys worry about it too much, and become dreamers.

But as T.E. Lawrence wrote:

All men dream: but not equally.
Those who dream by night in the dusty
recesses of their minds wake in the day
to find that it was vanity: but the dreamers
of the day are dangerous men, for they may act their
dreams with open eyes,
to make it possible.

BUCKET LISTS AND MELLIFLUOUS PLACE NAMES

A bucket list, made moderately popular in the eponymous film starring Morgan Freeman and Jack Nicholson, refers to things a person wants to do before she dies. Could be an activity (bungee jump), an achievement (write a novel), or, by far the most common, a place the person would like to visit.

I've been lucky enough to have ticked off many of the items on my bucket lists (getting to know my granddaughter, finding Hanuman's mountain in northern India, meeting folks who have captured white elephants, watching sea turtles hatch, trying to commune with an orangutan, spending time with pygmies in central Africa, hiking in the Darién Gap, speaking with the Sultan of Yogyakarta about the Mermaid Queen, and so on).

Most of my voyages involve purposeful travel – I do my homework first, make preliminary contacts with folks who might help, and set out to get the story.

But sometimes my travel strategy is less targeted. I find great appeal in visiting places with evocative names that vibrate with the smell of rough cooking fires and echoes of ghosts. The islands: Borneo, Sumatra, Flores, Kisar, and Andaman. The rivers: Mahakam and Mekong; Ayeyarwady, Chao Phraya, and Chindwin. And the cities, with tumbled buildings that could tell you of great battles, grand civilizations, and dreams (fulfilled and otherwise) if you just know how to listen: Surakarta and Rangoon. Malacca and Mandalay. Mahasarakham and Makassar. Where to stop? Mohenjo-daro and Siem Reap. Pondicherry, Penang, and Phitsanulok. Ulaanbaatar. And Luang Prabang – we must never forget Luang Prabang.

A dreamer hits the wall of reality.

BRUNO AND THE BLOWPIPES

Who will determine the future of Sarawak's isolated Penans?

BARIO, SARAWAK, MALAYSIA

The first time I came into contact with Penan tribesmen was in 1969. I was walking from Long Atip longhouse to Long Seridan longhouse, a trip that took us two days, with one night spent sleeping in the forest. It was late afternoon, and we were slogging across yet one more unnamed stream. I remember wanting to stop and splash around in the water to wash away the dirt and sweat of the trail, but the Kayan and Kelabit guys I was with wanted to carry on. Up another hill, down another hill. It was beautiful, in the monotonous way that the rainforest is beautiful, but I was too tired to pay much attention to the scenery. My memory at the time was, "What in the world did Tony Weng have for breakfast?" My friend Tony, a stocky Kelabit from Long Seridan, was lugging a forty-horse-power outboard engine on his shoulder, up the slippery paths, down the slippery paths, always good-naturedly, always without tripping, always with a grace and strength that made me envious of his skill and endurance.

We slid down an embankment to yet another stream and there they were. Five Penan men, ages ranging perhaps from twenty to forty. Three were wearing loincloths and two wore faded nylon sports shorts. Each man had a blowpipe and wore a hand-woven basket as a backpack. Their hair was cut in bangs in the front with a neck-length tail in the back.

They had probably heard us coming for an hour but had chosen to remain hidden until that moment, after they had decided that we were too bumbling to pose much threat.

My Kayan and Kelabit friends chatted with them for a while, and we gave them some provisions – tobacco, salt, some tinned food. And then they were gone, disappearing into the forest like sprites.

And the curious thing was that, at the age of twenty-two, I didn't give much special importance to the encounter. *Oh, we made contact with some Penans. Gee, I'm hungry.* That kind of thing. I had been in Sarawak for only a few months, working as a volunteer with the U.S. Peace Corps. It was all new and exotic, but at the same time I was becoming jaded. I didn't question that that semi-nomadic Penan we had just met wouldn't be around forever.

When we finally made camp, next to a clear, gravel-bottomed river, Tony waded toward a natural pool – I guess it must have been about two meters deep – and threw his nylon *jala*, a circular throw net, into the water. "Give me a hand to pull up the net," Tony yelled. His one throw had yielded about five substantial fish, each perhaps as long as my lower arm. He repeated the process a couple of times. "We don't need all those fish," I said.

"But the folks in the longhouse do. We'll gut them and smoke them so they last longer."

"And we can give some to any Penans we meet tomorrow," I said, feeling very generous with Tony's fish.

"If they bother to come back," he said. And then he added, enigmatically, I thought, "When they go hunting they can smell the animals. But the animals don't smell them. It's like they're invisible."

Fast forward some forty years. The Penans are in deep trouble.

Their ancestral land, the rainforest, is being cut for timber and then converted into oil palm plantations.

How serious is this deforestation?

Carnegie Institution for Science researchers estimate that eighty percent of the tropical landscape in Malaysian Borneo has been degraded by logging. The deforestation rate is accelerating faster than in any other tropical country, according to Sarawak Report, which suggests that some ninety-five percent of the primary forest has been damaged or destroyed.

The state of Sarawak is the richest in Malaysia; its people are the poorest.

PART OF THE DYNAMIC IS THE INTERPRETATION OF WHO owns the forest.

The Penans (today some three hundred Penans are considered semi-nomadic; the rest of the nine thousand are more or less settled) were hunters and gatherers and never made lasting farms. Because the legal definition of land ownership in Sarawak revolves around the ability to show a history of cultivation, the Penans could not make a convincing legal case that the land was theirs.

HELP WAS OFFERED FROM AN UNLIKELY SOURCE: A Swiss pacifist named Bruno Manser who lived with the Penans from 1984 to 1990 and championed their cause.

His Goliath-like opponent: Sarawak Chief Minister Tan Sri Abdul Taib Mahmud, a man who has made a ridiculous amount of money (some $15 billion, according to one estimate) by taking land away from his state's tribal people, cutting the forests, planting oil palm, and building huge dams that are unnecessary, poorly designed, and unsustainable.

From a distance it was an engaging fight, pitting a zealous foreigner fighting for the little guy versus a slight, silver-haired man with a goatee and a big appetite.

Up close it was nasty and, ultimately, depressing. A morality play that was immoral. As the endgame approached it looked like Goliath would withstand the stings of David's slingshot.

MANSER WAS DAVID WITH JOHN LENNON GLASSES AND an impish smile. He had a refreshing (some might say unrealistic) romantic streak. As a schoolboy in Basel, Switzerland, he wrote of living a back-to-nature existence: "If only I could one day travel to Sumatra, Borneo, and Africa and live like a caveman there in the deep, impenetrable jungle amidst gorillas, orangutans and other animals!" Even as a teenager he feared what impact uncontrolled development might have on the forests: "As a man, I would like to raze to the ground all the factories that are not vital. Instead of them I would bring to life a large forest with clear water and numerous animals."

As he matured he was able to realize his idealistic goals. He lived as an alpine shepherd seeking a cashless and liberated way of life.

And then he went to Sarawak and engaged in a Hemingway-like Big Life.

It's possible that Manser saw his story as a hero's journey, recognizing that the cause he had devoted so much energy to required an unforgettable epic hero. Manser did not shrink from the grand gesture to draw attention to the injustices he fought. In London he chained himself to a lamppost at a G7 conference. He parachuted into a crowded stadium during the Earth Summit in Rio de Janeiro. Manser went on long hunger strikes in Japan (at the headquarters of Marubeni, a leading importer of timber from Sarawak) and in Switzerland (to force the Swiss parliament to enact legislation against illegally traded tropical timber). He abseiled down a high-altitude cable car in the Alps, swam across treacherous rivers. He parachuted over the United Nations building in Geneva. He attempted to fly a motorized paraglider into Chief Minister Abdul Taib Mahmud's garden party, and he tried to buy four tons of 25-cm nails so the Penans could "monkeywrench" the valuable old-growth trees.

And throughout he wrote emotional calls to arms. When bulldozers came too close to his encampment, he climbed into the crown of a giant tree and wrote:

> When I behold the unspoilt valleys of the Seridan River – right up to the green swathe of the mountain ridges, where hardly any human foot has ever trod, I cannot stop the tears from coming to my eyes. Nature – you are Truth – even without human intervention ... And my heart cries like a funeral song – does this paradise really have to die and make way for chainsaws and bulldozers?

WITH MANSER'S ENCOURAGEMENT, THE PENANS blockaded timber company operations. Other hill tribes soon joined the fray since the same issues affect all of Sarawak's seven major upriver tribes, collectively called Orang Ulu, which includes the Kayan, Kenyah, and Kelabit communities where I had advised primary school teachers.

The blockades started tentatively, then gained momentum.

In March 1987 some four thousand seven hundred indigenous forest people created blockades that stopped sixteen hundred timber works from operating their two hundred bulldozers. A new wave of blockades in the autumn of 1989 involved some four thousand people.

These early initiatives drew public attention, but they were easily dismantled once the government lost its patience and called in the police to arrest the instigators.

Eventually the people of Sarawak realized the importance of lawyers, and today the multi-tribal blockades are linked to legal initiatives. In mid-2014 there were some three hundred court cases in Sarawak about land rights, and five active blockades protesting various land grabs. There were also two blockades to protest the Baram Dam, one of twelve proposed new dams that would inundate four hundred square kilometers of rainforest and displace twenty thousand people.

BRUNO MANSER DISAPPEARED IN BORNEO IN MAY 2000 at age forty-seven; he was declared dead five years later.

I MET MANSER SEVERAL TIMES. WE WERE NOT CLOSE, but I respected his understanding of the *realpolitik* that is at the heart of most fights between native peoples and paternalistic governments.

He achieved worldwide recognition from 1984 to

1990 when he lived in the rainforest with a band of semi-nomadic Penans. Malaysian officials saw him as a fugitive and a *provacateur* and called him the "enemy of the state number one." Manser constantly avoided arrest with the *panache* of a Swiss Robin Hood, zigging and zagging through the forest when police were on his trail, even once escaping after he had been captured. When he left Sarawak, through Brunei, he returned to Switzerland to create the nonprofit Bruno Manser Foundation. Bruno Manser, like other campaigners, said ultimate responsibility for the poor treatment that the state's indigenous people received was due to Taib Mahmud's greed.

DURING MY PEACE CORPS DAYS WE WOULD GO OUT AT night to hunt wild boar and more often than not return with a hairy pig on our shoulders. The rivers were clean, and jungle gibbons whooped their morning calls behind the longhouses.

On subsequent trips back to Sarawak, I was angered by the desolation of the landscape by timber operators and heard complaints from hundreds of people in dozens of longhouses. Their homes were being destroyed and they weren't getting anything for it. Fishing and hunting were terrible. The rivers had become treacherous, muddy and cluttered with debris from timber operations. I visited Penans who had been resettled into government-built longhouses, ugly structures with standard government-issue architecture similar to army barracks or timber camp housing. Tin roofs amplified the heat, making the residences uninhabitable during the day. The Penans I saw were listless, with vacant eyes. True, they now had access to basic health care and simple schools, but it seemed as if all the energy had been sucked from their thin frames.

When I discussed these issues with Malaysian officials, I got a standard defensive response, basically: "Don't tell us what to do, we know what's best for the Penans and the forests."

"Bruno Manser backed the Sarawak authorities into a corner by telling them what they should do," noted Chris Elliott, director of the WWF–World Wide Fund for Nature Forests for Life Campaign. "Even the slightest whiff of Western lecturing will put them on the defensive."

Perhaps it was a sloppy tactic – using Western-style confrontation to instigate policy changes in a proud Asian country.

During the height of Manser's long Sarawak escapade in the 1980s, Malaysia's prime minister, Mahathir bin Mohamed, had this irritable exchange of correspondence with young Darrell Abercrombie from Surrey, England.

Using his best penmanship (and unwittingly mirroring Bruno Manser's schoolboy essay), the boy wrote:

> I am 10 years old and when I am older I hope to study animals in the tropical rain forests. But if you let the lumber companys [sic] carry on there will not be any left. And millions of Animals will die. Do you think that is right just so one rich man gets another million pounds or more. I think it is disgraceful.

The prime minister replied on August 15, 1987:

Dear Darrell,

It is disgraceful that you should be used by adults for the purpose of trying to shame us because of our extraction of timber from our forests.

For the information of the adults who use you I would like to say that it is not a question of one rich man making a million pounds ...

The timber industry helps hundreds of thousands of poor people in Malaysia. Are they supposed to remain poor because you want to study tropical animals? ...

When the British ruled Malaysia they burnt millions of acres of Malaysian forests so that they could plant rubber ... Millions of animals died because of the burning. Malaysians got nothing from the felling of the timber. In addition when the rubber was sold practically all the profit was taken to England. What your father's fathers did was indeed disgraceful.

If you don't want us to cut down our forests, tell your father to tell the rich countries like Britain to pay more for the timber they buy from us ...

If you are really interested in tropical animals, we have huge National Parks where nobody is allowed to fell trees or kill animals ...

I hope you will tell the adults who made use of you to learn all the facts. They should not be too arrogant and think they know how best to run a country. They should expel all the people living in the British countryside and allow secondary forests to grow and fill these new forests with wolves and bears etc. so you can study them before studying tropical animals.

I believe strongly that children should learn all about animals and love them. But adults should not teach children to be rude to their elders.

PRIME MINISTER MAHATHIR DISCUSSED THE PENAN situation with Bruno Manser when they met at the 1992 Earth Summit in Rio de Janeiro. Less well known is that they had exchanged cranky correspondence for some six months.

In one letter Mahathir lectures Manser in a similar tone to that he used with Darrell Abercrombie, with the added spice of guilt and threats:

Herr Manser,

If any Penan or policeman gets killed or wounded in the course of restoring law and order in Sarawak, you will have to take the blame. It is you and your kind who instigated the Penans to take the law into their own hands and to use poison darts ... to fight against the Government.

As a Swiss living in the laps [sic] of luxury with the world's highest standard of living, it is the height of arrogance for you to advocate that the Penans live on maggots and monkeys in their miserable huts, subjected to all kinds of diseases ... Do you really expect the Penans to subsist on monkeys until the year 2500 or 3000 or forever? Have they no right to a better way of life? What right have you to condemn them to a primitive life forever?

You are trying to deny them their chance for a better life so that you can enjoy studying primitive peoples the way you study animals ... Stop being arrogant and thinking that it is the white man's burden to decide the fate of the peoples in this world ... Swiss imperialism is as disgusting as other European imperialism ... Stop your arrogance and your intolerable European superiority. You are no better than the Penans. If you have a right to decide for yourself, why can't you leave the Penans to decide for themselves after they have been given a chance to improve their living standards.

I GOT A GOOD LOOK AT THE TESTY DEFENSIVENESS OF Sarawak officials in the early 1990s.

I wrote a chapter on Malaysia's natural wonders for a coffee table book, *Malaysia: Heart of Southeast Asia*, the coordinator of which was Marina Mahathir, the prime minister's daughter. At an editorial committee meeting we asked the Malaysian advisors how candid we should be about environmental issues in Sarawak. "Tell the truth" they insisted. Easy for them to say – they were from Peninsular Malaysia, and isolated from the tetchy political realities of the distant and relatively independent state of Sarawak.

Someone (not me) wrote a photo caption in the book that really annoyed Sarawak state officials: "A logging road [not unlike the fictional one I describe in my novel *Redheads*] snakes along a once-forested ridge in Sarawak. Gunung Mulu [the national park as well as the mountain] in the background is now an island of green in a battlefield of dust and chainsaws." Another caption referred to "once crystal-clear waters" that "have become choked with mud and debris washed downstream from logging areas. The rivers have been further polluted by oil, chemicals, and other industrial and human effluent from timber camps located at the headwaters of many major river systems. This pollution has been a major source of conflict between Sarawak's lucrative logging industry and the native population."

These captions are accurate. They were also inflammatory and Taib Mahmud, the Sarawak chief minister who was going to launch the book in Kuching the day after the prime minister launched it in Kuala Lumpur, declared that he was instead going to ban the book. This led to a hectic bit of publishing diplomacy for Marina, and ultimately a compromise was reached. The edition sold in Sarawak would be reprinted, at significant expense, with the inciting photos and captions replaced by innocuous shots of people weaving baskets and giving each other tattoos. The irony is that six months after publication, Kuching's two leading bookshops – at the Sarawak Museum and the Kuching Hilton Hotel – were blithely unaware of the affront to the State and both proudly sold the original version of the book with the provocative photos and captions.

CERTAINLY CHANGE IS INEVITABLE FOR THE PENANS and the thousands of other, generally more sophisticated, indigenous people of Sarawak.

Who has the blueprint for that transformation?

Several years ago I consulted James Wong Kim Min, who was concurrently the Sarawak State Minister of Tourism and Local Government and one of the state's biggest timber tycoons, with substantial timber operations in Penan territory.

Wong loved to talk with foreigners about the Penans, whom he felt the foreign press had idealized as a group of innocent, downtrodden, blowpipe-wielding, loin-clothed rustics.

"I met with Bruno's Penans in the upper Limbang [River]," he said. "I asked the Penans, who will help you if you're sick? Bruno?" Here Wong laughed. "The Penans now realize they've been exploited. I tell them the government is there to help them. But I ask them how can I see you if you've blocked the road that I've built for you?"

I asked if he had a message for his critics.

> If [the West] can do as well as we have done and enjoy life as much as we do then they can criticize us. We run a model nation. We have twenty-five races and many different religions living side by side without killing each other. Compare that to Bosnia or [Northern] Ireland. We've achieved a form of Nirvana, a utopia.

I explained my experience with Penans who had been encouraged by generous government incentives to resettle into ramshackle longhouses. How their natural environment had been hammered, how their faces were devoid of spirit and energy, how they had seemingly tumbled even further down the Sarawak social totem pole.

In reply, Wong lectured me, as I have been lectured by numerous Asian officials when I raised similar concerns. In effect, he said, "We just want our cousins, the naked Penans, to enjoy the same benefits we civilized folk enjoy."

"We are very unfairly criticized by the West," Wong added. "As early as 1980 I was concerned about the future of the Penans." He cleared his throat and read me a poem he had written:

> O Penan - Jungle wanderers of the Tree
> What would the future hold for thee?
> Perhaps to us you may appear deprived and poor
> But can Civilization offer anything better?
> And yet could Society in good conscience
> View your plight with detached indifference
> Especially now we are an independent Nation
> Yet not lift a helping hand to our fellow brethren?
> Instead allow him to subsist in Blowpipes and clothed in Chawats [loincloths]
> An anthropological curiosity of Nature and Art?
> Alas, ultimately your fate is your own decision
> Remain as you are – or cross the Rubicon!

I GOT A GLANCE AT WONG'S "RUBICON" IN 2013 WHEN I visited Long Lamai.

Long Lamai (the term "Long" refers to the confluence of the rivers at which a settlement is located) can be termed a success story. Or a failure. Depends on which side of the Rubicon one chooses to stand.

This was the first large-scale Penan settlement village, created in 1955. It lies near the border with Indonesian Kalimantan. There are a couple of short longhouses, but many families live in solid individual wooden homes.

The primary school has been a success – the passing rate to enter secondary school was just four percent in 2010; that rose to fifty percent in 2012. After school there were always football games going on, both organized and not. Kids played volleyball and badminton and tag and just ran around being kids, all well fed, all bright-eyed.

The nearest clinic is an hour's boat ride; the nearest hospital requires a flight or an all-day drive in a four-wheel vehicle.

For church services, which the Penan here take seriously, mothers put ribbons into their daughters' hair, boys wear long pants, and the fathers put on socks and shoes. The service itself, at the Borneo Evangelical Church, is pretty dull stuff – a restrained pop band, lots of squirming kids eager to be released and head to the river to play. Flanking the droning preacher on the left is a picture of Jesus, on the right Santa Claus.

The Universiti Malaysia Sarawak, with a grant from the government of Japan, started a telecenter project to provide Internet service a few hours a week. Few people took advantage of this sporadic service.

More popular was television. I stayed in the home of the headman, Wilson Bian (one of a handful of homestays in the village), and, thanks to a satellite dish and a generator, the children of the household spent long hours watching popular Malaysian programs – the soap operas, the news, the Koran readings. They saw ads for Ding-Dang chocolate biscuits; watched programs like *Digista Teens Malaysia*, a pan-Asian series featuring teenaged creativity, and *Powerpuff Girls*, a Japanese animated series. All the cultural components of the new Malaysia.

Perhaps I exaggerate – they didn't watch with intent; they lounged on the floor while the TV was on, chatting, sleeping, and, once in a while half-heartedly trying to do homework.

The five hundred Penans of Long Lamai are mostly small-scale farmers, but the older folks enjoy (dare I say *need?*) to get into the forest to hunt and well, be Penans. The trouble is that a forest fire in 1991 burned the nearby primary forest, and wannabe hunters have to either walk two days to reach primary forest or hitch a ride on a pickup from a nearby village that sometimes heads in that direction.

Are they happy? Tough question to ask of any community. A few guys are active in the Penan protest movement – they organized blockades to protest abuse of tribal land rights, and to demonstrate against destruction of forest to grow oil palm and the construction of mega-dams. A lot of guys didn't seem terribly interested in politics except in a very practical sense – "we need better education, better health care" type of complaint. Fire in the belly isn't a phrase generally associated with the Penans. But what do I know about happiness? Or rebellion for that matter? I've never been forced to cross a Rubicon.

CHARLES HOSE, IN HIS CLASSIC 1912 BOOK *THE PAGAN Tribes of Borneo*, said:

> The Penans "in every way come up to the ideal of the "gentle" or "Noble" savage [with] something of the air of an untameable wild animal ... an honest and unselfish people ... and when once well-known they undoubtedly prove to be the best-mannered people of any of the savage tribes inhabiting [Borneo].

Discounting colonial terms like "savage tribes" (Hose, after all, was a British district officer in what is now Marudi, a gateway town to the interior), Hose makes a couple of observations that inform today's situation. The first is that the Penans were, what we might term "good people," without unsettling habits like headhunting. The second is that they were like a Rousseau painting come to life – everything we desire in a "Noble savage."

DURING MANSER'S TIME IN SARAWAK SOME OF THE Penans, but by no means all, became more confident, more vocal, less intimidated by authority. In addition to the blockades, they learned to speak in media-friendly sound bites. According to Bruno Manser's book *Voices from the Rainforest*, the Penans implicated the Kuching-based timber magnates when describing the vroom-whine of bulldozers as "the voice of the devils with the fat bellies." When a group of Kuching-based officials visited a blockade to attempt to convince the Penans to move to a resettlement camp, a nomadic Penan from Long Adang named Melai Beluluk taunted them: "Throw away your shoes, your shirts and take a blowpipe. Do you know the name of this river? This mountain? Which poison tree do we use for arrows? Do you know how to make sago?"

I was reminded of the eloquent plaints of Chief Seathl [Anglicized to Seattle] of the Native American Suwamish tribe who is reputed to have made an eloquent plea that the white man should leave the red man alone, since the Indian alone knows how to live as part of nature. Some skeptics claim that Chief Seathl's eloquent entreaties ("The white man does not understand our ways ... His appetite will devour the earth and leave behind only a desert ... Whatever befalls the earth befalls the sons of the earth.") were ghostwritten by the white missionaries who accompanied Chief Seathl on his lecture tour.

But the Penans were not railing against white colonialism. They were fighting against modern brown-brown colonialism.

When he heard about the troublesome blockades, Chief Minister Taib Mahmud replied, from the comfort of his Kuching office:

> I only want to help the Penans. Outsiders want the Penans to remain nomadic, and I won't allow this because I want to give a fair distribution of development to all communities in the state. We don't mind

preserving the Sumatran rhinoceros [an endangered species found in Sarawak] in the jungle, but not the Penans.

In reply, a Penan named Jemalan G, of Long Adang, said to a group of visiting officials: "You tell us to settle down and want to keep us under control like your water buffaloes and pigs. But what are you doing with them? You raise them and feed them only to finally cut their throats!"

THE PENANS ARE BEING HIT BY A DOUBLE WHAMMY.

The powerful men in the cities view them as low-status, semi-civilized rustics.

And, to the sophisticated urbanites, the Penans are perceived to live in a wilderness that is a place of demons, snakes, and disease. Put them together and you have a recipe for wanton environmental destruction.

Here's my argument.

This type of battle has been going on for as long as technologically developed people have confronted less technologically developed people. During the centuries of European colonial power, the Portuguese, Spanish, Dutch, Belgian, French, Germans, British, and Americans had little compunction against subjugating black and brown folks and taking what they wanted.

Closer to home, consider the "conquering" of the American West. The principle was that the educated and powerful decision-makers from the Eastern seaboard (old rich white guys) had a "Manifest Destiny" to civilize the Indians (convert them to Christianity if possible, exterminate them if they refused), slaughter the buffalo, and convert large swathes of wild forests and plains into more productive (and more "civilized") agricultural land.

Today that situation has morphed from white-brown colonialism into brown-brown colonialism. In Malaysia, for instance, government leaders and businessmen in the lowland cities of Kuala Lumpur and Kuching find it natural to be paternalistic toward their naked, darker, less-sophisticated brethren in the hills. For instance, Alfred Jabu, who is deputy chief minister of Sarawak and a member of the indigenous Iban tribe – the largest population group in the state – offered a familiar refrain: "We're giving them the chance to enjoy the same benefits other Malaysians have." It's a common litany: *We have to help our poor, naked cousins in the forests enjoy what we have.* The subtext: *We who live in the city are educated, well-dressed, speak the national language and believe in the national religion, have a responsibility to help the poor folks in the hills who might lack proper housing, education, sanitation and, how foolish of them, might not even know all the players of Manchester United. We have a manifest destiny, and opportunity, to give them religion and development. And all we ask in return is that they become good citizens. Oh, one more thing. We don't recognize their land claims for the forest they've been living in for centuries, so we'll go ahead and extract the valuable timber, burn what vegetation remains and plant oil palm. Don't they dare complain; it's not how civilized people behave. And especially don't complain to foreigners – that's unpatriotic. We're trying to build a nation here.*

Call it Social Darwinism if you wish. The implication is that the world is governed by a natural and inevitable progression of cultural development ranging from the most primitive at the bottom (Penans) to the top-of-the-social-totem-pole folks (powerful lowlanders in big cities) who imagine that they epitomize grace, culture, and learning.

This arrogance and greed becomes a deadly combination for both traditional culture and the natural environment. Once you disparage the Penan and the forest, you feel you have the right, even an obligation, to "civilize" the people and the environment. And devaluing the so-called jungle gives you a license to "conquer" the wild jungle, to exert your dominion over nature, and if you can make money out of the process, well, that's also your right.

SARAWAK OFFICIALS OFFER AN ECONOMIC JUSTIFICATION for cutting the forest, noting that ninety-five percent of the state's substantial oil revenue and eighty-five percent of the natural gas revenue goes to federal coffers, leaving Sarawak little choice but to earn money from natural products, of which timber is by far the most profitable. "Where are we to get money except through the forest?" asked James Wong Kim Min, former Sarawak Minister of Tourism and Local Government and one of the state's leading timber concessionaires.

And there is a lot of money to be made.

Malaysia is the world's leading exporter, by far, of tropical logs, tropical sawn wood, and tropical veneer, and second, after far-larger Indonesia, of tropical plywood.

Today Malaysian companies run timber operations and plywood mills as far afield as Guyana, Suriname, Papua New Guinea, and the Solomon Islands according to a report by Nigel Sizer, of World Resources Institute and Dominiek Plouvier, an independent forestry consultant.

TAIB MAHMUD GOES FROM STRENGTH TO STRENGTH. On February 12, 2014, he resigned as Sarawak chief minister (and finance minister, and resource planning and environment minister), only to take up a post three weeks later as governor. His successor as chief minister, Adenan Satem (who is Abdul Taib's former brother-in-law), has de facto become Taib Mahmud's business manager and continues the old man's policies. Questioned about the need to build environmentally damaging dams, which displace thousands of villagers, Satem replied: "If we have to build more dams to generate electric power for the industry, we have to build more dams whether the environmentalists or non-governmental organizations agree or not."

He neglected to mention three pertinent facts, however. The first is that the rivers belong to the people of Sarawak. The second is that there is angry opposition to the various dam projects on social and environmental grounds. The third is that it is the Taib Mahmud family that stands to make the most money out of the construction and related land grabs.

INTERNATIONAL PRESSURE HASN'T DONE MUCH GOOD. In 2014 Malaysia rejected a suggestion at the United Nations that the UN Special Rapporteur on Indigenous Rights should be allowed to visit the country and evaluate the treatment of the Orang Ulu. They insisted they will not comply with the UN Declaration on the Rights of Indigenous Peoples or ensure that Native Customary Rights (NCR) are protected. However the Malaysian government promised to create a "Task Force" to look into the problem.

HAS MANSER BEEN SUCCESSFUL?

From a public-awareness point of view he directed a modicum of global media attention to the plight of the Penans and other tribal groups.

But he failed at his major objective: getting the Malaysian government to declare a biosphere reserve to protect the Penans and their primary forest. In an article in the newsletter of the Bruno Manser Foundation, the activist admitted "success in Sarawak is less than zero."

Chris Elliott, a WWF executive who met Manser several times, agreed that the future isn't bright for the Penans and their forest home. "There is severe pressure from unsustainable logging, forest fires, and conversion to plantations," he said.

Manser had a cautious relationship with the conservation mainstream. No doubt he felt that groups like WWF were too soft.

"We differ on the means," Elliott admitted. "WWF tried to work in partnership with the government and had some success – a few protected areas were established, there was training of staff, and new wildlife legislation was created. But neither Manser nor WWF succeeded in getting the authorities to create a biosphere reserve."

History isn't made by people who follow the rules. Manser sensed a major injustice and challenged the status quo in which his friends the Penans were paternalistically treated as the least important, least powerful members of this multicultural society.

So, how will the Swiss man be judged by history? As an obstinate fighter or a romantic visionary? A winner or a loser?

What motivated this middle-aged man from rich Switzerland to live six years in the forest of Borneo with virtually nothing that most people would consider essential? He learned to process food from the starchy sago palm, learned to hunt with a blowpipe, learned how to live a life that was simultaneously ridiculously hard and unimaginably rewarding.

He recorded their stories and wrote a dictionary – the Penans have thirteen hundred expressions and names for the plants of the forest.

And throughout he continued to dream, writing of his epiphany:

It happened in a prison in Lucerne. I was imprisoned there for three months because I had refused to learn how to shoot at human beings. One day I suddenly perceived the space inside the four walls of my cell ... how my body acted as a biosphere ... to be so small and yet so incredibly rich and important ... [I] flew out of the prison, over to my parents in Basel, to my friends in Amsterdam ... I flew on and left our solar system. Then I turned around and flew back. There I sat, back in my body. Since then I carry this certainty in me: every one of us is nothing and simultaneously the most important creature in its space and place. Indispensable from the first to the last breath. So when people say: "don't be active, it's just a waste of time, it won't help anyway," then you already know that they're scared of losing profit and would even sell their own grandmother. Does it have to be the children today who dare say out loud to the politicians and the economists: support what is real and true, avoid what is bad!

WHAT MIGHT HAVE HAPPENED TO BRUNO MANSER?

I have several theories, all of which depend on what we know about Manser's last days, and what we might surmise. Whichever theory you subscribe to (or make up on your own), Manser's fate is destined to become an unsolved Asian mystery, like Michael Rockefeller's 1961 disappearance in the Asmat region of New Guinea or the 1967 disappearance of Thailand-based silk entrepreneur Jim Thompson in Malaysia's Cameroon Highlands.

We know that in May 2000, after crossing the

unmarked forest border from neighboring Indonesia, Manser walked to the large Kelabit settlement of Bario. He carelessly stayed at the Penan rest house where he could have been spotted by any number of people.

Carrying a 30-kg pack, Manser left Bario on May 25, 2000, accompanied by his Penan friend Paleu and his son. Near Bukit Batu Lawi, a two-thousand-meter limestone pinnacle considered sacred by the Penans, Manser said he wanted to climb the mountain alone and made plans to meet up again a few days later.

Manser had previously suggested to his Swiss friends that this was going to be his last trip to Sarawak; he was tired of the fight and despondent that the Penans, uncomfortable with confrontation, hadn't taken on more of the responsibility. Manser had almost died in a failed attempt to climb Bukit Batu Lawi a few years earlier, and scaling the peak would have been a fitting finale to his grand Sarawak adventure.

So, what might have happened?

One possibility is that he had an accident during the climb of Bukit Lawi. He might have fallen. He might have been bitten by a snake. He might have broken his leg and been attacked by a clouded leopard. But his body was never found, nor any of his effects.

Or two possible conspiracy theories.

The first is that someone saw Manser in Bario and told Malaysian security forces. They followed him into the forest and once he was alone they tried to capture him. Manser had been captured once before and had escaped, to the chagrin of the army, and perhaps this time he tried to escape once again. During the confusion they shot him, accidentally or not, and instead of having the messy situation of a prominent dead European to deal with, the security forces simply buried him in the rainforest.

The second conspiracy theory has similar dynamics. Someone saw Manser in Bario and told someone in one of the timber companies working in the area. The timber companies paid some thugs a few hundred dollars to get rid of him.

Some five years after his disappearance, on March 10, 2005, Manser was declared legally dead by Swiss authorities. His Penan friends claim he simply "disappeared."

THE "DISAPPEARING" HYPOTHESIS IS BASED ON Manser's despondency that his efforts on behalf of the Penans had not yielded results.

Before he left for his last trip to Sarawak, Manser asked a German friend and protégé to carry on his work in the event he did not return.

Manser sent some four hundred postcards to friends and family from Indonesian Borneo before re-entering Sarawak, something he had never done previously (in one postcard he complained of diarrhea and a broken rib). While in Bario he wrote a letter to his girlfriend Charlotte in which he said he was "very tired."

The expert Penan trackers who searched for him could find no trace of his body, thereby putting into question the theory that he had had a fatal accident.

If he had been killed by police or timber assassins, wouldn't it be likely that someone involved would have gossiped to friends and the secret would have gotten out?

None of these notional clues (and that's all they are) prove that Manser killed himself.

But some people who knew him, who ask not to be named, suggest that Manser had bought into his own legend. He had named the foundation he set up after himself. As an only child, he was used to making himself the center of attention – in public he was self-effacing but not shy about taking center stage. He felt conflicting emotions. On the one hand he was frustrated and felt he had failed his Penan friends, not living up to his own vision of himself as a savior of the oppressed. On the other hand he sensed the need for drama, which only he could provide.

And what do the Penans think?

There is a scene in a 2014 film about the Penans called *Sunset Over Selungo*, made by a Swedish TV crew, which atmospherically shows the early-morning mist rising over the rainforest treetops. When a group of Manser's Penan friends in Sarawak saw this scene, they said, "that mist that protects the forest is Brother Bruno."

Manser had become more than a martyr. He had become a myth.

A tourist boat gets caught in the "Yellow Streak" during the 2012 Benak Festival.

SURFING WITH SOMERSET

Riding the "Yellow Streak" where Maugham almost died.

MANDALAY

omerset Maugham never mentioned the crocodiles.

Sure, he wrote about his near death when his boat capsized in a tidal bore in Sarawak, and he used that incident in his story "The Yellow Streak."

But no mention of gigantic, hungry reptiles, which were on my mind as I clambered into a canoe, preparing to ride the tidal bore on the Batang Lupar river. I felt certain that if we capsized, I could swim to safety, or at least hang on to the overturned boat. But I had no illusions that I had any defense against saltwater crocs.

ON APRIL 25, 1921, IN ONE OF HIS LONGEST AND most interesting letters from Asia, Maugham wrote about the drama he and his companion Gerald Haxton experienced:

On the way down river we had a most unlucky experience. They have on some of these Borneo rivers what is called a bore, a tidal wave several feet high that comes roaring up with the change of the tide. It is well known to be very dangerous and great precautions are taken to avoid it. But by some mischance we met it at the most dangerous part of the river [and at] the most dangerous time. It was a wall of seething roaring water eight feet high that burst upon us and before we knew where we were, we were all struggling in the water. We had a crew of prisoners who were paddling us down and they shouted to us to cling to the boat. This we fortunately did because we have heard since that with the undercurrent in that stormy sea of waves it would have been impossible to reach the shore. The boat began to turn over and over, and we struggled like squirrels in a cage to cling on until at last we got absolutely exhausted. I don't know what we should have done if it had not been for the two malay [sic] prisoners who managed to get a wet mattress to us when we were just about all in. Fortunately by then we had drifted a little nearer the shore and so with their help were able to reach it. I cannot tell you how good it felt to feel that slithering mud under one's feet. We lay on the bank for about half an hour absolutely exhausted until a paddle boat came along and took us off. We were all as near drowning as anyone could be and when we got back to Kuching, the capital of Sarawak, found our escape looked upon as almost miraculous.

I wanted to ride the tidal bore, locally called a benak, in a small dugout canoe, partly for the adventure, and partly because Maugham is one of my favorite writers and I wanted to follow, modestly, in his footsteps.

I had been in touch with Anthony "Yep" Colas, a prominent French stand-up paddleboarder who was the first person to surf the Sarawak tidal bore. Colas, who has ridden many of the world's four hundred tidal bores, called the Batang Lupar bore "among the top five in the world."

I checked the tide tables in the Sarawak Almanac and noted the dates and times of the King Tide, which generates the benak. The height and power of the benak varies greatly, ranging from the size of the wake of a small motorboat to a frothy rolling wave of muddy water (which Colas dubbed the Chocolate Factory) that can approach a height of almost two meters. Some of the tides took place during the night, obviously not a good time to swim with crocodiles. Due to the limits of my travel schedule, I blocked out a few days in November 2014.

I took a comfortable bus from Kuching to Sri Aman, a quiet town of twenty-six thousand some sixty kilometers upriver from the South China Sea. The tidal bore is central to Sri Aman's tourist positioning — it calls itself "The Benak Town" and sponsors an annual Benak Festival.

There I enlisted the help of David Ho, a local photographer and paddleboard enthusiast who has actively documented and promoted the tidal bore on the Batang Lupar river, where Maugham's adventure took place.

David, in turn, engaged Jemat anak Entering, a sixty-three-year-old Iban from nearby Rumah Assan on the Temelan Ulu river, who owned a suitably flimsy boat.

I was ready for a big adventure, something of sufficient magnitude to enthrall my granddaughter Ranya Apsara with admiration for my bravery.

Of all the tales of big crocodiles emanating from the Batang Lupar, one legendary individual opens its jaws wider than the others. This is the croc known as Bujang Senang. The name Bujang Senang is Malay for "jolly bachelor" and I find it a bouncy moniker for a huge, dangerous reptile. But according to James Ritchie, who wrote *Man Eating Crocodiles of Borneo*, the term "senang" doesn't refer to "carefree and contented" but to the Senang River, a tributary of the Batang Lupar. Bujang Senang, he says, is an immortal "white spirit" crocodile that feeds on humans in retribution for human "warfare" against other crocodiles.

Ritchie estimates that at least twenty-five people died due to crocodile attacks in Sarawak during the period roughly spanning 1945 to 2000. Some of the crocodiles were later captured, and his book is full of photos of animals more than four meters long and weighing more than two hundred kilograms. The humans posing next to the dead animals look insignificant and vulnerable.

(Globally, saltwater crocodiles kill one hundred sixty-eight times more people each year than sharks, according to one estimate. Statistics are hard to come by, partly because crocodiles often attack in isolated regions where reporting is difficult, while shark attacks generate significant news coverage.)

Ritchie recounts details of some of the attacks:

It was hot and muggy on the afternoon of June 26, 1982. Bangan anak Pali and his brother Kebir went fishing for prawns. Bangan was in a good mood; he had just been appointed chief of his longhouse. But as he and his brother started out on their fishing trip an omen bird, which can be good or bad depending on the circumstances, crossed their path.

In retrospect Bangan anak Pali and his brother should have turned back. But they continued to the muddy and shallow riverside, and Bangan stepped on a log to steady himself while he fixed his net. Suddenly there was an explosive sound and Bangan screamed as a big crocodile attacked. His elder brother Kebir jumped in and grabbed the crocodile around the mid-section, but this feeble effort was unsuccessful and the crocodile thrashed once and swam away. Bangan's mauled body was found five days later.

The Sarawak Almanac *told me that the tide on November 22, 2014, would occur at* 16.54 *and reach* 5.8 *meters.*

"That's the height of the tide, it's not the tidal bore," David Ho explained. "Don't expect big waves." He saw my disappointment and didn't try to sugar-coat the reality. "If you want waves like in the photos, you should come back in April or May. I gave David a copy of Maugham's story and explained that it was in April when Maugham had his adventure. David nodded. "Sure, the benak *can reach two meters then."*

Never mind, I thought. It'll still be an adventure and Ranya Apsara gives me unconditional love, so I'll be okay.

THE CROCODILES OF THE BATANG LUPAR HAVE LONG intrigued international researchers.

Conservationist Jeffrey A. McNeely recalls a case involving the disappearance of two east European scientists who had visited the river to study the crocodiles. Making their camp on an isolated, nipah-palmed riverbank, the eager researchers set out their remote-controlled cameras, using chickens as bait to tempt the large reptiles into video range. However, one evening a pair of crocs decided they preferred human meat. After the researchers had been missing for several days, Sarawak police were called in to investigate. They in turn called in a very different type of expert – a noted crocodile magician named Abdullah bin Buaya – who promised to entice the man-eating crocs into a cage by singing a magical chant. Abdullah captured two animals, a female and a male. On cutting open the first crocodile, Abdullah was able to confirm that "the female crocodile ate the Pole." And what about the other scientist? the police asked. The crocodile magician answered confidently, "The Czech's in the male."

Seen from the air, the Batang Lupar, like all of Sarawak's rivers, winds like spaghetti from its origin in the mountains that divide the Malaysian and Indonesian parts of Borneo. By the time it gets to Sri Aman, the river is half a kilometer wide, a bit sluggish and the color of greenish café au lait. Outside the town area, the population decreases and the banks of the river are verdant with coconut trees and smallholder gardens. We take the boats a couple of kilometers downriver. The mud on the riverbank is viscous and I sink to my knees when I climb out of the boat to have a pee.

Jemat has come in the requisite small boat, called a prahu, about as long as an adult crocodile and made of fiberglass. But it has a small engine. I complain to David, reminding him that I wanted a Maugham-like experience.

No problem. It's not a proper outboard but a small engine that sits inside the boat and drives an external long propeller. Jemat takes the contraption apart, throws the pieces into the bigger support boat, and we set off into the middle of the river.

"It's coming in ten minutes," he says. I don't see anything but soon hear the distant sound of a muffled freight train. Far on the horizon I see a line of white on top of the gray-green water, a study in aquarelles.

In fact, the entire afternoon is awash in pastels. It's overcast and the light is like a soft-focus filter smudged with dust.

The wave approaches and we get in position. It's like surfing. When it's nearly upon us, Jemat tells me to start paddling hard so that our speed matches that of the wave. The benak is only about sixty centimeters high, at most, but we are able to surf the wave for minutes at a time. Once in a while we don't hold our line and are turned sideways, but the wave isn't large enough to capsize the boat. Jemat quickly puts us right and we carry on. It's a bit of a rush, surfing on Maugham's benak. The pastel haze parts briefly and lets in a bit of afternoon sunlight, and the froth of the benak takes on a touch of golden hue. Maugham's done it again, I think, creating a double-meaning title.

"THE YELLOW STREAK" BORROWS LIBERALLY FROM Maugham's own experience. In the story an old Borneo hand, Izzart, has been ordered to escort a visiting mining engineer named Campion on a survey to the interior of Borneo. They were polite to each other, but Campion, a prim man who cared about appearances, was somewhat uncomfortable by Izzart's "broken and discoloured teeth ... his khaki shorts were ragged and his singlet torn ..."

Maugham adds:

> [Izzart] was very sensitive to the impression he made on others, and behind Campion's joviality he had felt a certain coolness ... he was exasperated by the possibility that this common little man did not think entirely well of him. He desired to be liked and admired ... He wished the people he met to take an inordinate fancy to him, so that he could either reject them or a trifle condescendingly bestow his friendship on them.

Near the end of their uneventful few weeks in the forest, a bit tired, a bit dirty, and a bit bored with each other's company, they "hankered now for chairs to sit on and a bed to sleep in." They were keen to enjoy civilized British company (and civilized British gin).

Heading downriver, just a day from the river mouth where they would meet the coastal steamer that would take them to the capital of Kuala Solor (Maugham's name for Kuching), their *prahu*, paddled by strong-shouldered local lads, gets caught in the tidal bore. The story is reported from Izzart's point of view and he tells of his complete panic as the boat "went round and round and they scrambled over it like squirrels in a cage," just as Maugham himself experienced. Izzart hears Campion's cry for help, but instead saves himself, with the help of one of the Iban boatmen.

Izzart struggles ashore, glad to be alive. To his surprise Campion shows up, very much alive, a few hours later.

Like the heroes in much colonial literature, Izzart carries a terrible secret. His mother is Malay, and he is terrified that his half-caste status, "that wretched drop of native blood," will become known to the pure white British officials with whom he lives and works. How many times has he himself said "everyone knew you couldn't rely on Eurasians." And in this case, they couldn't; Izzart had cut and run.

Of course there's a twist in the end, like in most of Maugham's stories.

My afternoon on the river ends calmly. No mishaps, no life-threatening situations, only mild excitement. And no crocodiles. I hadn't expected any.

"Do many people catch crocs these days?" I ask David.

"They're a protected species," he says.

"But they're good to eat," I say.

David is law-abiding, though, and doesn't take the bait. We leave it at that. I find it curious that it's the normal scheme of things when a crocodile eats a person, but in modern Sarawak it's illegal to reverse the situation and fry up a chunk of croc meat with ginger and spring onions. The men in Maugham's colonial Sarawak stories wouldn't have stood for such an imbalance of the natural scheme of things.

A harem, a sure sign of an ambitious king.

"The Harem Beauty" (1918) by Henri Adrien Tanoux.

KRUMBLING KRATONS

Searching for the first white rajah of Borneo
and other sultans, kings, and wannabe royals.

uick quiz for students of Asian history: Who was the first white rajah of Borneo?

No points if you answered James Brooke, the Englishman who was appointed Rajah of Sarawak in 1841 and who started a three-rajah reign that lasted until 1946.

The first white rajah of Borneo was the Englishman Alexander Hare, who had his moment in the Borneo sun some thirty years before James Brooke.

I sought to follow Hare's trail, but few people had heard of him, for he left no monuments, no lasting social innovations, no glittering palaces. What he did leave were hundreds of illegitimate children and many thousands of miserable slaves.

Alexander Hare was an English trader who was sent to Borneo in 1812 by Stamford Raffles, the Lieutenant-Governor of British Java, to become Political Commissioner of the Government for the Native States in Borneo, and Resident of Banjarmasin.

Among the historians who bother to study him, Hare was either a talented diplomat who secured a strategic treaty with an important sultan, or an egocentric, law-breaking wastrel who used his position to service his own needs.

In his reports Raffles praised Alexander Hare, saying that under his administration Banjarmasin had been "reduced to order and regulation." Raffles effused that Hare was "a gentleman whose desire after useful knowledge and whose zealous exertions in the cause he has undertaken, are perhaps unrivalled."

Not so, according to Tim Hannigan, author of *Raffles and the British Invasion of Java*: "The truth was that under Hare, Banjarmasin was reduced to poverty, disorder and unprofitability."

The British managers reported that Hare "had been received at the Sultan's Court with the most particular respect and attention, and had been hailed throughout his Highness's [George III] dominions as the deliverer of that once powerful Kingdom."

Not true, according to historian Graham Irwin, who wrote that Hare was "plausible, unscrupulous, and ambitious [and whose] desire was to found a kingdom of his own where he could luxuriate in oriental splendour surrounded by slaves and ladies of the harem."

But Raffles stood up for Hare, and noted that the strategy to engage the sultan had been Hare's and there was not "any other person competent from local knowledge, and from respectability of character to whom the charge could have been entrusted."

Was appointing Hare a brilliant tactic or something Raffles would privately regret?

The general consensus is that appointing Hare was one of Raffles's least successful management decisions. According to Hannigan, Hare was guilty of "unhinged despotism, flagrant disregard for British colonial law, and outright sexual excess."

Alexander Hare's legacy led to two phrases that are jolly sound bites in British colonial history. Hare's excesses, oversized testosterone surge, and outrageous chutzpah led to a colonial embarrassment known interchangeably, take your pick, as the Banjarmasin Enormity and the Banjarmasin Outrage.

What did Hare do to deserve such colorful vitriol?

He engaged in the slave trade. He did not pay any duty on his own trade and was accused of using the salt monopoly for his own profit. He charged the running costs of his shaggy kingdom to the British crown. And then there were the girls. Oh my.

Alexander Hare's kingdom was located an easy hour's drive south of Banjarmasin, a rambling city of some six hundred thousand in southern Kalimantan.

With Gusti Marhusin and Yudi Riswandi, relatives of

the Sultan of Banjarmasin, I drove along a good two-lane road. It is a flat, gormless region of floodplains and muddy rivers, just a step upgraded from a swampy morass, with rice paddies and rubber gardens providing background to the on-road commerce that one finds throughout Indonesia – motorcycle dealers, small restaurants offering duck rice, a few shops, not much of anything. And, like elsewhere in Indonesia, motorcyclists with the road sense of gerbils weaved in and out of the sparse traffic, spewing litter in their wake.

Hare had settlements in Tatas, where the official post was first located, then a settlement at Pulo Lampai, later a more fertile site called Kurau (where he tried to construct a canal that would cut a line from the plain around Kurau to the Maluka River).

Modern residents know nothing of this period of local history.

We visited the village of Maluka, the namesake village of his scruffy kingdom, where the main historical landmark is a disused airstrip built by the Japanese during World War II.

In a comfortable wooden house we met Muhammad Hanafiah, 74, who was delighted to have visitors. His face reminded me of the American comedian Drew Carey. As with everyone we met on the road that day, his personal grooming was spotless; he wore a clean brown and cream long-sleeved batik shirt and tan pants. I felt underdressed, wearing a faded batik shirt and beige nylon trekking pants. Hanafiah was hard of hearing and we had to repeat our questions as we sipped sweet tea while sitting on strips of flower-patterned linoleum brought out for our comfort. He was generous with his hospitality but couldn't offer much help in the search for Hare. The ladies of the household, however, a rural version of the kind of attractive middle-aged women that the British term "yummy mummies," joined in, curiously all dressed in shades of purple, and they agreed we might find some clues farther down the road in the village of Tabenio.

Alexander Hare (1775–1834) was an English merchant who joined a trading company in Portugal around 1800, moved to Calcutta several years later, and promptly set up housekeeping with a fourteen-year-old dancing girl named Dishta.

He later settled as a merchant in the Malaysian port of Malacca, where he met Stamford Raffles (sorry, this gets confusing; the Malaysian city of Malacca has no relation to Hare's territory of Maluka in Borneo – sometimes written Moluko – or the far-eastern Indonesian Molucca Islands – also known as the Moluccas). Hare had already exhibited his proclivity for young women, and Raffles biographer Tim Hannigan says that in Malacca Hare ran "a highly irregular household with barely post-pubescent Asian women of various races tumbling out of every bedroom."

Pubescent Dishta is a tantalizing character, but she might not have existed. The few historians who bother to write about Hare mention her as true. However it seems she might have been created by a Dutch novelist whose fiction was translated into Indonesian and then into English, and then she morphed into the category of "unchallenged truth." But Dishta is such a delectable character that I will continue to include her in this tale, with the warning that she might be just a figment of the imagination, an enigma of sloppy scholarship.

During the 1811–1816 British Interregnum, when England took over Java from the Dutch (who were busy losing battles closer to home against Napoleon), Raffles responded to a request from Sultan Sulaiman al-Mutamidullah of Banjarmasin for help in suppressing lawlessness and piracy (similar to the reasons the Sultan of Brunei sought the assistance of James Brooke some three decades later). Raffles saw the opportunity to establish a strong trading relationship with Banjarmasin, located on the southern tip of the island of Borneo, and appointed Hare to establish the bond.

The sultan welcomed Hare and gave him a chunk of swampy, unproductive land six times the size of Singapore.

It was hardly a salubrious base, but Hare wasn't picky and he set himself up as ruler of a personal kingdom called Maluka, issuing his own coinage and indulging in a personal business that was, in word if not deed, illegal in British-controlled Indonesia: slavery.

He also indulged in his predilection: young women. Lots and lots of young women.

Shortly after Hare arrived in Banjarmasin, he immediately broke East India Company policy and Raffles's own regulations for British residents at native courts. A resident was not supposed to accept any kind of gift from a king, including gifts of land. (Perhaps trying to distance himself from Hare, Sultan Soleiman later complained that Hare's land was meant to be used for his private residence, and was not intended to house unruly convicts who frightened the local citizens.)

And the women running around servicing Hare, well, that just wasn't the way British colonial officials were expected to behave.

A few kilometers along the road from Maluka village we reached Tabenio, a village set on the river of the same name, which is the site of a Dutch fort. I started to walk toward a hillock, all scraggly grass with a cow and a few goats slowly grazing. There was no monument, no excavation, no remains of a battlement. Nothing. The only way to identify the area as an archeological site was by reading the faded signboard put up by the Indonesian department of archeology.

I started to walk around the site. My travel companion Gusti Marhusin had just been promoted to a senior civil service position and he was conscious of village protocol and basic Indonesian etiquette. "Better wait here," Marhusin said. "We'll go ask permission of the village head if we can look at the site."

My friends left; I ignored their caution and strolled

around the hillock, trying to imagine whether it was here that Hare had his base. The nearby river was about forty meters wide, and a dozen fishing boats were stranded on the mud of the outgoing tide. Yes, this quiet village, with its easy access to the sea, could easily have been the site where Hare waited impatiently for new shipments of slaves and women to arrive from Java. There was little to see, so I strolled around the village and returned an hour later to the hillock. Gusti Marhusin had just returned. "Do we have permission to see the site?" I asked. "I suppose so," Marhusin said. "The headman wasn't around."

Walking around Tabenio village, set amidst vast areas of not-very-much, whose primary interesting features were the river and the fishing boats, I thought of the lost European "lords" about whom Joseph Conrad wrote so incisively: white men with shady backstories who achieved a modicum of success in isolated Bornean villages, largely due more to their skin color than their innate wisdom or skills, men who have taken "native" wives who neither understand nor love their husbands, men who are re-spected to their faces but mocked behind their backs, men who are constantly asked to finance their wives' extended families (and my, they had no idea how broadly their new families extended), men who dream of returning to England, or to Holland, or to wherever, anywhere really, as long as they get out of the fetid, swampy morass in which they grit out a living. They are men with dreams who nevertheless see the reality – they will never leave but will die upriver and be buried in a grave that will flood with the first monsoon rain and be all but forgotten by the next rice harvest.

Stamford Raffles, famed for his subsequent "founding" of modern Singapore, whose PR suggests he was a liberal and visionary colonial administrator and a staunch advocate against slavery, was Hare's primary enabler.

According to Hannigan, Raffles signed "an order that all convicts in Java were to be shipped to Banjarmasin for Alexander Hare to do with them as he saw fit."

Hannigan adds: "But the supply of convicts was not enough for Hare ... He wanted more people, and in particular, he wrote to Raffles, he wanted *women*. He was especially interested in women of 'loose morals.'"

Raffles agreed, noting that it was essential "to the tranquillity and improvement of a new Establishment that the Population should bear a due proportion of both sexes ..." To achieve this utopian goal, Raffles ordered authorities to procure young women to move to Maluka, either voluntarily, or in exchange for release from debts they or their families had incurred. One might suspect that even if a woman could not be identified as having "loose morals," she might be rounded up on the pretext that she may exhibit such tendencies in the future.

We don't know how many people Raffles shipped out to Hare's fiefdom. "Certainly they numbered in the thousands," estimates Hannigan. Post-Raffles the incoming British administrators calculated there were nine hundred and seven men, four hundred sixty-two women, and one hundred twenty-three children living in Maluka, all a result of Hare's initiatives and Raffles's interventions. An unknown number had died, fled, or accompanied Hare when he decamped to South Africa.

Why did Raffles go against his oft-praised progressive instincts?

One theory is that Raffles knew the British Inter-regnum was just that, a temporary period of British influence, after which Holland would come back to reclaim the territory it had ceded to Britain. The ambitious Raffles thought that Hare's feudal outpost, plus Hare's friendship with the powerful Banjarmasin sultan (the second most influential Malay ruler in littoral Borneo, after the Sultan of Brunei, far to the north), would assure a strong British outpost deep within Dutch territory, which would give the British a bargaining chip in the likely event the Dutch would return.

Raffles's instincts proved correct. Historian David Oats wrote:

> The Netherlands had been liberated, and the British Government felt that a strong and friendly Nether-lands would help keep the French, long-standing adversaries of the British for key Asian territory, in check. Britain decided to restore to the Dutch some of the colonies they had held prior to the start of the European conflict and on 13 August 1814 a convention between Britain and the Netherlands was signed, which allowed Britain to retain possession of the former Dutch colonies in South Africa and Ceylon, but

restored to the Dutch all the possessions in the Eastern Archipelago [Indonesia] that had been conquered since 1803.

I'm fascinated how major powers traded strategic and distant territories like young boys might trade baseball cards; witness the earlier seventeenth-century Treaty of Breda between England and the Netherlands in which England traded the tiny eastern Indonesian island of Run, source of nutmeg, for the similarly unimposing island that became Manhattan, source of beaver skins.

Hare had the exuberance of a puppy and the gift of gab, charm, and self-confidence of a born con man. But the women, what's that all about? It's both hard and risky to theorize about a man's sexual appetites by reading historical accounts written more than one hundred fifty years ago, by people who were hardly neutral. Contemporary writers of psychohistory are forced to filter a few historical facts through their own prisms into generalizations about a person's personality. Hare had huge harems. That's a fact. But was Hare more a Hugh Hefner-type, who got power and perceived status by having women hanging around, or a Don Giovanni-wannabe with an insatiable sexual appetite? In the end it hardly matters. He cultivated harems the way some men grow roses, and that characteristic annoyed plenty of people.

Of course sex harems have been a perk of royalty since monarchs were first created, and it can become a numbers game to determine which ruler had more damsels at his disposal. King Kashyapa of Sigiriya in Sri Lanka had a harem with as many as five hundred women. In Mexico, Aztec ruler Montezuma II, who lost his empire to Hernán Cortés, kept four thousand concubines. Sexual excess sometimes went hand-in-hand with cruelty. Sultan Ibrahim the Mad, a seventeenth-century Ottoman ruler, is said to have drowned two hundred eighty concubines of his harem in the Bosporus. And a fifteenth-century Ming ruler ordered twenty-eight hundred concubines, servant girls, and eunuchs who guarded them to a slow, slicing death as the Emperor tried to suppress a sex scandal that threatened to humiliate him. Both examples suggest that the monarchs had plenty of other women left in reserve.

Alexander Hare, by comparison, played in the minor leagues.

When the Dutch returned to Indonesia in 1826, Hare was forced to leave. He packed up his harem and sailed to South Africa, where he was quickly evicted by moralistic colonial officials. He bundled up his estrogen-rich household once again and moved to one of the most isolated spots on the planet, the tiny group of uninhabited coral atolls called the Cocos (Keeling) Islands, lying in the middle of the Indian Ocean, far from both meddling colonial bureaucrats, but also far from any sources of new concubines to provide amusement or slaves to provide income.

Hare was eventually pushed out of Cocos by a Scottish sea captain, John Clunies-Ross, at one time an employee and friend of Hare's.

Clunies-Ross disapproved of Hare's lifestyle and resented having to share the tiny territory, observing that Hare was "a worthless character" who was guilty of "atrocious lying" and was "as wicked as Satan himself could have desired."

Having gotten rid of Hare, Clunies-Ross then emulated Hare by proclaiming himself King of the Cocos Islands. In 1886 Queen Victoria granted the islands in perpetuity to the Clunies-Ross family; they were subsequently transferred to Australia in 1955.

Women in tow, who perhaps were getting a bit tired of the constant change of scenery, Hare left once again, some say for Singapore, others say for Batavia (modern Jakarta). What we do know is that he died in 1834 in Bencoolen, Sumatra. And, if you wish to believe it, the remnants of his estate went to the one person who had stayed by his side (or whom he had chosen to keep around) during his peripatetic wanderings: Dishta, the perhaps apocryphal dancing girl from Calcutta who by this time was a mature forty-something woman.

TWO TYPES OF PEOPLE START THEIR OWN COUNTRIES and make themselves rulers: the grumpy bastards and the irrational dreamers.

How many times have I lost patience with stupid drivers, with people on the bus who don't offer their seats to pregnant women. People who play awful music loudly, who commit genocide, who wastes taxpayers' money, who traffic in women, and who sell AK47s to militias made up of twelve-year-old boys. People who rape and pillage their countries' rain forests, who abuse natural and tribal rights. People who don't see anything wrong with the American Second Amendment. Don't get me started. People who wear backward baseball caps, especially indoors. People who let their children jump on the seats in trains and restaurants. Like the Lord High Executioner in *The Mikado*, like Santa Claus, I've got a little list.

But on the positive side, why not create a *better* society? Where children are encouraged to color outside the lines, where there is peace and love (but without the syrupy, self-indulgent need for a religious rationale), where kids reaching puberty have clear rites of passage to adulthood, where the punishment fits the crime.

And my role? King, to be sure. Or maybe Grand Nabob? Supreme Alchemist? Absolute ruler, but fair, a wise and clear-thinking soul when the situation calls for it. Benevolent despot.

Try it yourself. Create your own country. You'll need to make some executive decisions. What will be your job? Type of government? National anthem (mine would be "Jumpin' Jack Flash")? National fruit/mollusk/snack food (Indonesian satay)? Tourist slogan ("If you can find us, you'll love us")? Who will be given citizenship? Who not? Will your country be accessible in Mittel Europe and active in the global community of nations or hidden away on some tropical island?

SOME ROYALS HAVE A CLEAR IDEA OF WHAT THEIR ideal nation might look like.

Nancy Valerie Brooke was the third daughter of Charles Vyner Brooke, the third (and last) of Sarawak's "White Rajahs," whom reporters dubbed "The Siren of Sarawak," and "Princess Baba." She dreamed of buying an island in the Netherlands East Indies (Indonesia) with her professional wrestler husband to be called "Babaland," where, according to Valerie, "every man would be Rajah." In his book *Sylvia, Queen of the Headhunters*, Philip Eade quoted Valerie as saying, "We're going to have a democracy, but with a court and things – maybe an aristocratic democracy. I think a country without lots of uniforms and braids is no fun."

ONE OF THE SADDEST SCENARIOS IS TO BE A RULER without a country, like the royal family remnants of Italy, Romania, Greece, and Albania who live in genteel poverty in Geneva.

Any ruler worth his (or her) salt needs a country.

The good news is that it's remarkably easy to create a new country, and in doing so, declare yourself king/sultan/emperor/Big Kahuna.

I love the idea of starting your own country. I propose something similar in my novel *Earthlove*, in which a nature conservation organization thinks about buying a tropical archipelago and establishing a Republic of Rich Misunder-stood Heads of State to provide secure luxury housing, with a passport, for deposed dictators who otherwise might face pesky legal efforts to divest them of their fortunes. Instead of wandering around the world seeking asylum, Baby Doc could have leased an island of his own, as might have Ferdinand Marcos, Idi Amin, Mobuto Sese Seko, and other rich despots.

But can you start a new country just like that?

Well, countries are being created and destroyed all the time. The United States, of course, didn't exist before 1776. Italy didn't exist before 1866, and even then it was missing Rome, which joined in 1870. A vast swath of African and Asian countries were mere pink blotches on the colonial maps before the post-World War II period, and the 1990s breakup of the Soviet Union and Yugoslavia created nation-building opportunities for many territories that previously were only known to stamp collectors. The United Nations had just one hundred fifty-seven country members in 1981, but this number expanded quickly – South Sudan became the one hundred ninety-third UN member state in 2011. Palestine and Tibet? Watch this space.

MOST NEW COUNTRIES ARE CREATED BY STANDARD CAUSES – wars, revolutions, political uprisings, collapse of empires.

But when does an almost-nation become a genuine-nation?

This question was put to Englishman Roy Bates, who,

in 1967 reinvented himself as Prince of the Principality of Sealand when he took up residence on an abandoned World War II anti-aircraft tower off Britain's east coast.

When questioned by BBC whether Sealand is in fact a nation, Prince Michael, Roy's son, said, "We've never felt the need to ask for recognition [by other countries]. You just have to fulfill the criteria of the Montevideo Convention, which is population, territory, government, and the capacity to enter into negotiation with other states."

The Montevideo Convention on the Right and Duties of States, accepted by one hundred ninety-eight signatory states, and adopted by the League of Nations in 1933, says that any entity that meets all of the criteria can be regarded as sovereign under international law, *whether or not other states have recognized it.*

BUT DON'T DISCOUNT HUMAN INGENUITY IN THE nation-building process. These examples might not meet the criteria described above, but they certainly illustrate the energy of the wannabe rulers.

* For $145 you can become a citizen of the Principality of Castellania in Austria, where Prince Ralph I, formerly a *burgher* named Otto Hubner, has sold more than two thousand citizenships in twenty-five years of independence.

* In November 1998, Philippines police raided a hotel in Olongapo, near Subic Bay, and arrested a

Briton, an Australian, and a Malaysian. They had been running an Internet scam that offered passports for a fictitious nation called the Dominion of Melchizedek, named after Jerusalem's high priest who blessed Abraham after Abraham rescued his nephew Lot and his family from Sodom. The Dominion of Melchizedek's bubble burst when a man who identified himself as "His Serene Highness Gerald-Dennis Sayn-Wittgenstein-Hohenstein" tried to open bank accounts in Hong Kong with checks issued by phony Melchizedek banks. The twenty-two-year-old unemployed Austrian, who had been living in the passenger terminal at Kai Tak airport in Hong Kong, turned out to be a baker, not a prince. During his trial it was learned that he had visited a number of Asian countries with his Melchizedek "diplomatic passport." He was convicted for bank fraud and jailed for six months.

* In the geographical United States you could become a citizen of the Republic of Roadkills-R-Us, whose motto is "Tread on Me."

* In 2015 a Czech named Vit Jedlicka proclaimed the new republic of Liberland on seven square kilometers of land that was previous *terra nullius*, unclaimed by either Serbia or Croatia – a quirk of an ongoing border dispute between the two former Yugoslavia countries. One attractive provision in the nation's proposed constitution "significantly limits the power of politicians so they could not interfere too much in the freedoms of the Liberland nation." Applications for citizenship are accepted only by email, since Liberland does not have a post office.

* Maharishi Mahesh Yogi tried to create the Global Country of World Peace.

* Most young girls play at being princesses, but seven-year-old Emily Heaton's father decided to make her a real princess. Jeremiah Heaton, who lives in the American state of Virginia, searched online for unclaimed land, finding Bir Tawil, an arid region on the border between Sudan and Egypt that nobody seemed to want. In 2014 he obtained permission from Egyptian authorities to travel to the rocky patch of desert, some twenty times larger than Manhattan, where he planted a blue flag with a crown and four stars and (rather unimaginatively, for my taste) named it the Kingdom of North Sudan. "I founded the nation in love for my daughter," he said. Jeremiah Heaton says he's confident that the African Union will welcome him and the Kingdom of North Sudan, even though neither he nor his family have ever lived in the nation. Princess Emily shows signs of becoming a visionary ruler; she wants to make the kingdom into an agricultural production center.

ANOTHER ROLE MODEL IS LAWRENCE W. SWAN, AN American biologist specializing in ecology of the Himalayan region, where he searched for the jumping spiders of Everest, the springtail fly, and the ever-elusive yeti (which he concluded was a large mountain fox whose peculiar hopping gait left footprints that appeared to be those of a biped). He had the distinction of discovering two new species and having them named after him: a Himalayan frog, *Rana swani*, and a flea found only in glaciers, *Machilanus swani*. More to the point of this chapter, Swan once "seceded" from both the United States and Redwood City, California, protesting the order that he replace – at his own considerable expense – his "perfectly adequate and more efficient septic tank" with neighborhood sewer lines.

He anointed himself "Raja" of his own autonomous native-state – the Kingdom of Cooch Nahai – meaning "absolute no have" in Hindustani, or the State of Absolutely Nothing.

As the *San Francisco Chronicle* reported:

> Fortunately, [Swan] made a concession to the government's right of eminent domain and continued to pay his taxes. But that did not stop him from providing Cooch Nahai with everything a small country needs. Cooch Nahai printed its own stamps – an annual philatelic issue containing the image of a forgotten element of natural history. It had a national holiday, June 21, the summer solstice; a national

symbol, the extinct Dodo [sic] bird; its memorial tomb of the Unknown Frog; and its Great Wall of Cooch Nahai, which contained mementos of global travels and conquests.

IN 2015 LEADERS OF TWELVE MICRO-NATIONS ATTENDED A global summit of like-minded visionaries – MicroCon 2015, held in Anaheim, California, near another putative-state, Disneyland.

MicroCon 2015, which should not be confused with the thirty-ninth MicroCon, the Annual Conference of the Indian Association of Medical Microbiologists, was hosted by His Excellency President Grand Admiral Colonel Doctor Kevin Baugh, the founder and current president of the Republic of Molossia. His house and garden near Reno, Nevada, form the nation's territory, population twenty-seven, which boasts a flag, stamps, currency, customs, radio show, and post office.

Baugh's advice for people who want to start their own nation:

> First off, use your imagination. It's not necessarily all an imaginary thing, but it does require you to think outside the box when you're starting your own country. Learn about what other nations do. You know, learn a little bit of history – how countries have started and eventually stopped. And then, of course build it from what you know. Your flag should represent you and your country – your coat of arms, all that kind of thing.

MY FAVORITE SELF-DESIGNATED ROYAL IS JOSHUA Abraham Norton, a nineteenth-century English Jew who sold supplies to San Francisco gold rushers and then declared himself Emperor of America.

In 1859 Norton walked into the offices of the San Francisco *Bulletin* and presented them with this single sentence, which they ran on the next edition's front page:

> At the preemptory request of a large majority of the citizens of these United States, I, Joshua Norton ... declare and proclaim myself Emperor of these U.S., and in virtue of the authority thereby in me vested to hereby order and direct the representatives of the different States of the Union to assemble in Musical Hall of this city, on the 1st day of February next, then and there to make such alterations in the existing laws of the Union as may ameliorate the evils under which the country is laboring, and thereby cause confidence to exist, both at home and abroad, in our stability and integrity.

It was signed "Norton I. Emperor of the United States."

Norton I had a common touch: he abjured seclusion and luxury, attending every public function by foot or bicycle. If he noticed someone performing some kind act, he might spontaneously ennoble them, from which practice the expression "Queen for a Day" was obtained.

In return for his noble generosity, restaurants offered the emperor free dinners, he was given three seats at every theatrical performance (one for himself and one each for his famously well-behaved dogs, Bummer and Lazarus). The city itself paid for his uniforms, and Bay Area newspapers published his proclamations. Norton issued his own currency, which was widely accepted (and which today is sought after by collectors – in early 2015 a fifty-cent note of the Imperial Government of Norton I dated March 11, 1876, was offered for sale at $8,800). He had a habit of levying taxes by walking into the offices of an old business friend and announcing an imperial assessment of ten million dollars or so, but could quickly be talked down to a cigar and small change. When he was arrested by an overzealous policeman "to be confined for treatment of a mental disorder," virtually every newspaper published editorials denouncing the action and Norton was released with a lengthy public apology from the chief of police.

Some of his ideas were visionary: he proposed the formation of a League of Nations and the building of a suspension bridge between San Francisco and Oakland. Norton sent frequent cables to fellow rulers offering well-informed advice. King Kamehameha of Hawaii (then the Sandwich Islands) was so taken with the Emperor's insight and understanding that toward the end of his life, Kamehameha refused to recognize the U.S. State Department, saying he would deal only with representatives of Norton's Empire.

When Norton I died in 1890, ten thousand people lined up to view his mortal remains; his funeral cortege was three kilometers long. At 2.39 p.m., during his funeral, San Francisco experienced a total eclipse of the sun.

ALEXANDER HARE'S KINGDOM WAS BASED ON A MACHO view of life. The Anti-Hare country is The Other World Kingdom, a feminist resort/micro-nation in the Czech Republic, with its own currency, passports, police force, and courts. Its goal: "To get as many male creatures under the unlimited rule of Superior Women on as much territory as possible." To become a citizen "a woman must own at least one male slave."

HOW DOES A PERSON BECOME KING SO-AND-SO THE First?

The key elements seem to be a military victory, a Texas-sized ambition (with a big dollop of cruelty), patronage of other senior leaders (and skewer 'em if they don't acknowledge your great power), plus a really good magician (think Merlin) or PR agent (Karl Rove). A good biographer is useful as well, somebody like the anonymous Chinese hagiographer who wrote of a Ming dynasty warrior emperor: "Full of spirit and brimming with energy, imposing in appearance and bold in speech ... of iron and stone were his liver and bowels. His mind probed strategies and tactics that neither demons nor gods would fathom ... "

But that recipe is missing a mystical element. I'd suggest that a King Numero Uno should quickly establish a link with appropriate divinities, gods, and spirits. Perhaps through dreams, perhaps through omens. Create a suitably mystical and imposing backstory and much of the job is done. The best example is King Bhumibol Adulyadej of Thailand, the world's longest reigning monarch. He is referred to as Rama IX, and the use of the name "Rama" clearly positions him as an avatar of Vishnu, thereby linking him with both Rama (of *Ramayana* fame), who was the seventh avatar of Vishnu, and with Buddha, who was Vishnu's ninth avatar. To consolidate the symbolism, King Bhumibol's royal emblem features the godlike sunbird Garuda (*Krut* in Thai), which is Vishnu's mount. When one sees the Thai *Krut* on a government building, it signifies that it is under the protection and control of the Vishnu-related king, literally "the king/ Vishnu is in the building."

ONE OF THE PERKS OF BEING A KING IS THAT HE CAN award honors to friends and loyal followers, thereby (hopefully) ensuring their future fealty.

For a while I toyed with the idea of becoming a knight, but my unconsummated fling with royalty did not come through the beneficence of a reigning monarch. It came from a classified ad nestled between tiny announcements promising "Beautiful Russian girls want to meet you" and "Lucrative business opportunities in West Africa."

I TURNED DOWN A KNIGHTHOOD. IT WAS A TOUGH decision – I liked the sound of "Sir Paul."

I had replied to a notice in the *International Herald Tribune* that had offered "an economically available, State Sanctioned Hereditary Knighthood."

Turns out that some wannabe nobles have resurrected the Knights Templar, a prominent and powerful group of medieval Christian noblemen who protected pilgrims on the crusader routes to Jerusalem.

The Knights Templar were created by the Catholic church in 1127 and were wiped out the same way, when Pope Clement V's bull *Vox in excelso* of March 22, 1312, abolished the group, despite its being vigorously championed by celebrities such as Dante Alighieri. Two years later the Church ordered Knights Templar Grand Master Jacques de Molay burned at the stake.

The literature surrounding the Knights Templar weaves historical fact, fantastical tales, conspiracy theories, metaphysics, and religious geopolitics. Some writers claim that the image of what is now called the Shroud of Turin is actually Jacques de Molay's. An abundant shadow literature claims that the Knights Templar were the origin of Freemasonry, that they had links to the fabled continent of Atlantis, that they possessed the Ark of the Covenant and the Holy Grail.

Several years ago a group of mostly British visionaries recreated the Ancient and Noble Order of Knights Templar as a nonprofit organization in Israel. For just a single $5,000 fee, and fees of $500 year (less than my golf club fees), I could be honored in an investiture involving *apanages* and escutcheons. I'd get to wear a special ring and have use of two castles and the opportunity to buy privately bottled Knights Templar Bordeaux.

And even better, the title comes with citizenship of a new country they're creating, code-named Savantis.

"Only five people know where it is," said Knights Templar Chancellor Savant Graham Renshaw-Heron. But from reading between the lines, I figure they're buying an island in the Philippines or the Caribbean. According to Sir Graham, the thousand or so locals are enthusiastic about becoming Savantists and living under five dukes who will control the country. The nation will become a beacon of hearty, mostly British-bred, capitalistic enthusiasm, with economic benefits accruing from the planned casinos, resorts, golf courses, offshore banking, and flags of convenience shipping.

I asked my friend Dan about whether he too wanted to sign up – I figured we could get a two-for-one deal, maybe even a free toaster.

"Those guys don't need their own country," he said. "They're already on their own planet."

The Knights Templar certainly have a history of geographical expansion. The medieval group had a fleet larger than that of most countries – Columbus flew the Templar's red cross on his sails. William Mann, author of *The Labyrinth of the Grail*, claims that the Knights Templar "possessed the 'secret' of being able to fix longitudinal positions long before it became common practice," and that this "sacred geometry" had allowed Neolithic- to Roman-era "societies who were in on the secret to circumnavigate the world and settle corners of the world that are far removed from Europe."

Savantis, Sir Graham assured me, was "just an inch away from receiving United Nations recognition." I could see myself as social director at the Savantis Golf Club, perhaps, or professor of creative writing at Savantis University.

One thing is sure, though, and that is there will never be a Gay Pride Day in Savantis. The Knights Templar constitution, which preaches that "there are no, nor shall there ever be, any political, religious or racial affiliations, obligations or favours of any nature," draws the line on the issue of homosexuality. They are very clear: "While it may be recognized that certain governments, and for their own reasons, have de-criminalized acts of homosexuality, it is the avowed policy of this Noble Order to unreservedly condemn and decry all such activities."

Homosexuality is a leitmotif in Knights Templar history. After his arrest on the morning of October 13, 1307, de Molay spent the next seven years in prison undergoing extreme tortures to force him to issue a confession that would damn the order in the eyes of the people and the Catholic Church.

Although de Molay confessed under duress to denying Christ and trampling on the Holy Cross, he steadfastly denounced the accusations that the initiation ritual consisted of homosexual practices.

I don't much like the idea of Savantis telling people how to run their lives. Nevertheless, I grudgingly admire the Knights Templar's fighting spirit, encouraging the "abandoning of all wimpish thoughts whether this or that cannot or should be attempted."

The Knights Templar documentation is whole-heartedly individualistic and appeals to anyone who thinks there is entirely too much government in our lives. Savantis will be a libertarian place where:

> Further and more self-evident human rights such as the absence of oppressive alimony laws, childish seat belt laws, alcoholic consumption laws, the punishment of success by the successful being forced to support the unsuccessful, or the energetic being obliged to support the slothful, shall also be Constitutionally and con-spicuously absent, while the inherent rights of self-defence, privacy, protection of property, etc. shall be immutably enshrined in The Constitution of Savantis, which shall become blended with the Constitution of this Noble Order ... "

It's their right, of course, to decide who can become a Savantis citizen and what the codes of ethics are. North-ern Australia, among many places, prohibits homosexuality. Vibrators and sex toys are outlawed in Kansas. And adultery will, theoretically at least, get you arrested in New York.

When I questioned the civil liberty issue, Sir Graham argued, "Your golf club wouldn't allow me to play in just a bathing suit. They're allowed to set their own standards of behavior. So are we."

I didn't like the possibility that these guys, and they're all guys since women can't hold Savantis office, could conceivably change the constitution in a few years and tell me, say, that the Missionary Position is the only approved posture.

But I like the sound of Sir Paul. The truth is, I was tempted. I left myself a phone message ("Sir Paul, this is Steven Spielberg. I'd like to make a film of your novel.") to see how it sounded. It sounded just fine. (I'm rather used to honorifics, actually. My mom called me Angel. My wife calls me Hunk. Other acquaintances have called me more colorful titles.)

But I've always rejected honors. I refused to join the high school honor society. I refused to join a fraternity. With the exception of my golf club, I'm sympathetic to Groucho Marx's rejection of any club that would have him as a member.

But still, "Sir Paul" has a certain ring (and a reasonable price tag). Maybe I was too hasty. Maybe I could work my way up the Templar totem pole. Since I'm a writer, I could eventually be known as "The Prince Formerly Known as Artist."

<hr>

I HAD NAÏVELY THOUGHT THAT CHINA'S 2,000-YEAR-old imperial system ended when twelve-year-old Pu Yi, the last emperor, was overthrown in 1912.

"Not so," declares Elmer. "*I'm* the last emperor."

I met the man I'll call Elmer, for reasons that will

become clear, by chance. He stood next to me in front of the visitors' board at the East-West Center in Honolulu. "There are some Chinese visiting," he observed sotto vocce, as if he was speaking in Spy vs. Spy code.

We began to talk. Elmer was suspicious at first. He is Chinese and royal. I am Anglo and common.

Elmer is obviously an emperor of the people. Plain gray T-shirt. Dirty jeans. Flip-flops. Black hair, speckled gray, pulled into a ponytail. His briefcase was a folded piece of cardboard, from which he extracted a complicated genealogy, linking him directly and definitively, he explained, to the tenth-century Zhou dynasty as well as to Chou En-lai, Sun Yat-sen, and Chiang Kai-shek.

But what about Prince Aisin Giorro Pu Jie? I asked, referring to the younger brother of Henry Pu Yi, the last emperor whose life was featured in Bertolucci's film. The eightysomething-year-old Pu Jie lived in an old house a stone's throw from the Forbidden City in Beijing; he died in 1994 at age 87.

"Pu Yi was Ching dynasty. Manchurians. Invaders. My family are *real* Chinese," Emperor Elmer said.

His genealogy, printed on the back of his CV, told a contorted tale of usurped emperors and invaders, and of exiled royalty who emigrated to Hawaii. Shaky about Chinese family trees, I asked around and found that Elmer has been a bit, er, creative, with his historical narrative. One scholar thought the emperor "learned his history from a fortune cookie."

But hey, call me a dreamer. What if I invited Elmer for

lunch, figuring that, just in case he was who he said he was, it couldn't hurt to be pals with the Big Guy.

Elmer ordered chop suey from the University of Hawaii's cafeteria. I had a hamburger.

Elmer wasn't too clear about his strategy for gaining the throne. He wants to visit China, for the first time, to see his people. "Can you find funding for me?" he asks. He wants to bring Western ideas to the Middle Kingdom, particularly the religion of the Jehovah's Witnesses. "Chinese are Semites," he explains obliquely. "Direct descendants of Noah."

I suggest it might be useful for American-born Elmer to learn a few phrases of Mandarin. "Uh?" the emperor-to-be grunts, which is the way he acknowledges new, seemingly apparent ideas, as in "This is how you network."

"Uh?"

He bridles at the suggestion that he also might brush up a bit on Chinese politics and customs. He gets edgy. I've overstepped his royal space.

I ask him, respectfully, I hope, what qualifications he has to lead 1.2 billion people.

Elmer waves the genealogy. He went to college for four years but left before getting a degree, muttering "It was a fake sexual harassment case." He adds: "I'm stable, level headed. Have good common sense. I hope it's tough for someone to take advantage of me."

He doesn't think China is ready for a democratic movement. What about the current generation of Chinese leaders? "They're doing the best they can."

"President [George H.W.] Bush had about the right kind of China policy," he adds. But he's down on Henry Kissinger. Elmer points out that he once handed a letter to Kissinger, who was visiting Honolulu, asking for support. To Elmer's surprise, Kissinger spent all his time in Hawaii without seeking the emperor's counsel about how Sino-American relations would improve once Elmer took over the throne. So much for Kissinger's renowned geopolitical acumen.

Elmer could use some heavenly miracles since his claim to the throne is in danger of disintegrating unless he gets some support.

Elmer explains that he has high-placed relatives in the Hawaiian political and social world. "But they won't help me," he says. "They're jealous. Afraid of my power. And the CIA wants to assassinate me." I agree not to use his real name.

We meet a couple of other times but since Elmer has no phone and no fixed domicile, it is difficult to set up appointments.

Although we lose contact, I read about China's political travails with renewed interest. Could it happen? Improbable comebacks happen all the time in sports and politics. Emperor Elmer. He's tanned, rested, and ready. Emperor Elmer. I like the sound.

CHINA'S HUGE, BUT CAN IT HANDLE TWO EMPERORS?
Kamal Ashnawi also claims to be Emperor of China.

And he's Emperor of Indonesia. A prince of India and Thailand. And the world's richest man.

Journalist Philip Golingai, who interviewed Ashnawi in 2012, described him as wearing a baseball cap and a long-sleeved shirt and jeans. Just a normal guy who was born in Perak State in Malaysia on January 1, 1964.

I sought out Lord Kamal, as his staff refer to him, but he hasn't yet responded to my phone messages, SMS texts, and Facebook (649 "likes" at the end of 2014) communications. So my knowledge of his life and dreams is gleaned from press reports.

He was raised in a "very simple and ordinary" family in Malaysia but pursued his higher education at Dartmouth College in the UK (marine engineering) and further study at Delft University of Technology in the Netherlands. He has experience in the oil and gas industry and has mentioned a plan to create a world-class petroleum industry hub in Malaysia.

As Golingai relates, "it was in Holland in the late 1980s that Kamal found out who he really was when a member of an Indonesian royal family, kicked out of the country by President Sukarno, told him he was of royal blood."

In the early 1990s a lawyer told Kamal about his royal family's massive wealth. The two flew to Kunming in China where, Golingai reports, they "hiked up a mountain for four hours and reached a cave guarded by an old couple who, Kamal says, are immortals."

He found the "wealth of the dynasties that ruled China" – stacks of gold bars, jade, and diamonds.

Kamal claims to be the reincarnation of Emperor Nurhaci (reign: 1616–1626) the founding father of the Qing dynasty of China.

Kamal says that his royal wealth is kept in secret accounts in some one thousand banks worldwide, and notes that "86.7% of the world's money belongs to me." In a press conference in Kuala Lumpur, Malaysia, in 2013, Kamal revealed bank documents from HSBC that could not be authenticated by the journalists present, but that he said showed he was worth some 6.4 trillion euros. To put that number in perspective, 6.4 trillion euros (roughly $7.8 trillion) would make Kamal a thousand times richer than Bill Gates, and worth more than the combined economies of Germany and France – a fortune equivalent to approximately 8.5% of the world's GDP. In the website he set up to describe his fund management vision, Kamal Ashnawi noted that he wants his wealth to be used to "bury poverty," improve health, improve education, and promote something he describes as "life upgrade."

Kamal Ashnawi is incredibly rich. Alexander Hare was poor. But they do have one thing in common.

In a blog published in *The Warmonger Report*, Kamal is quoted as saying he enjoys the attention of "eight *dayangs* [female attendants] to cater to his needs and that once he is crowned as Emperor of Indonesia, he will engage eight hundred *dayangs*.

Noblesse oblige.

KRUMBLING KRATONS KWIK KWIZ

Question: *Who was the first White Rajah of Borneo?*

Answer: You're not paying attention; go back and reread the chapter.

Question: *What modern country has more sultanates and kingdoms than any other?*

Answer: Indonesia.

Although there are no authoritative counts, researcher Donald Tick estimates that there are more than three hundred royal lines still existing, in various forms, throughout Indonesia, with some one hundred ten of them found in the small islands of eastern Indonesia. Some fifteen of those sultanates can be found in Borneo. I met three of Borneo's sultans, but that's the theme for another book.

Question: *Which countries share the island of Borneo?*

Answer: Brunei, Indonesia, and Malaysia

Question: *What illegitimate grandson of a famous Scottish poet was expelled from Sarawak in the 1850s and tried to set himself up as a king in North Borneo? Among his controversial policies: arms trading, stealing women, and encouraging local tribes to kill anyone trying to* compete in his self-proclaimed territory. Hint: His death (beheading by pirates) was avenged by Jane Austen's brother.

Answer: Robert Burns Clow

Question: Who was responsible for Britain gaining control of Java in the nineteenth century?

Answer: Napoleon, who defeated the Dutch, thereby forcing them to cede their Indonesian territories to the British

---

Question: What four states have existed, more or less intact, from Year Zero to the present day?

Answer: Ethiopia, Mauritania, Albania, and Armenia

Question: Name the writers who created these fictional white rajahs:

1. Daniel Dravot and Peachey Carnehan, who sought to become kings of Kafiristan, in The Man Who Would Be King
2. Kurtz in Heart of Darkness, set in central Africa
3. Eugene Henderson, the Wariri Rain King in the African nation of Sungo

Answers:

1. Rudyard Kipling
2. Joseph Conrad
3. Saul Bellow

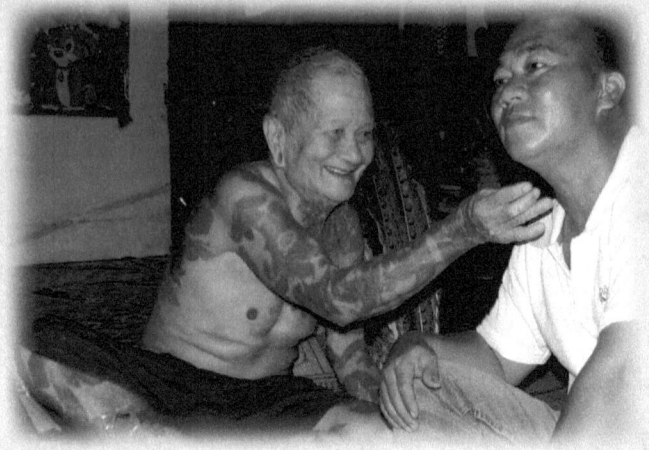

Good bedside manner – Unding anak Libau treats a patient.

THE (ALMOST) LAST SHAMAN

It's been a good ride, but Iban healer doesn't expect many others to follow his path.

SERUBAH ULU, SARAWAK

o the untrained eye he seems an unlikely magician. Frail, but with a hundred-watt smile. He has two wispy whiskers, short gray hair, and holes in his earlobes where he once inserted teeth from a wild boar. He walks a bit slowly. But cut him some slack. He's ninety-one, thereabouts. He's got tattoos on his neck, his arms, his legs; he's not much different from most elderly Iban men. Except unlike most men, Unding anak Libau can chase spirits and make ill people healthy.

Unding anak Libau is a *manang*, a traditional healer, living in a longhouse in Sarawak, not far from the Indonesian border. He's one of the last of his profession.

NO ONE KNOWS HOW MANY IBAN *MANANG* ARE LEFT. While the Iban tribal group are in no danger of dying out

– they comprise some thirty percent of Sarawak's population – the number and influence of *manangs* like Unding is dwindling due to easily discernible dynamics, linked like Olympic rings.

I met with three senior Iban academics at the Tun Jugah Foundation in Kuching; one of their objectives is "To preserve and promote Iban culture, arts, and language." Tan Sri Leonard Linggi Jugah, who is director of the foundation, Robert Menua Saleh, and Peter Kedit explained the realities of modern life that threaten the existence of people like Unding. There's the availability of Western education. Fluency in English and Bahasa Malaysia to complement the Iban language. Ease of transport, which means people can easily travel far from their longhouses and mingle with other people and cultures – marriage between Ibans and folks from other ethnic groups is common. Communications – it's rare to find a longhouse without TV, cell phones, and often Internet. Easy access to hospitals and clinics. Enough money to enjoy the consumer economy.

PERHAPS THE MAIN REASON WHY THE *MANANG* CULTURE is dying is because of that pervasive force of anti-Animism: Jesus Christ.

Religion can be a tricky subject for many families, and it's no different when Unding sits down with his family. In 1979 Unding's son, Galau anak Unding, had a dream. He saw two women in white shirts. They saw some ghosts and prayed while holding candles. The ghosts ran away. Galau interprets this as meaning that the two women were Christian and that the Anglican religion can protect people from ghosts.

Galau converted and asked his father to also become a Christian. Unding had his own dream, however, in which Unding's personal spirit guide, the *nyigit* or cicada, appeared and told him that if he became Christian he would soon be invited to "go join the spirits." For Unding this was a clear message that if he converted he would die. While Unding stayed with the old beliefs, he doesn't mind that a Christian cross (a simple dark blue one) is displayed on the front door of his apartment in the longhouse – after all, Christians live within and they're family. Galau, for his part, has become the longhouse's lay preacher.

FOR THE VISITOR THE IBANS ARE GREGARIOUS AND hard-drinking, always ready for a party.

And for visitors to Sarawak, a night in an Iban longhouse is a memorable souvenir.

Even today, in our supposedly enlightened world, sophisticated people (the kind of folks who dislike the term "tourist" and refer to themselves as "travelers") are intrigued by esoteric customs and costumes. The government-run Sarawak Tourism Board invites visitors to spend the night with descendants of Iban headhunters, and tour operators are not shy about promoting images of tribal folks wearing loincloths, vests made of clouded leopard skin, and caps adorned with hornbill feathers. The dramatic and photogenic folks a visitor sees during an Iban cultural show wave machete-like parangs while stomping about on the bamboo floor of a scenic longhouse.

When I first lived in Sarawak, in 1969, many rural riverine longhouses had little sanitation. The river offered you a toilet, as well as a place to wash your clothes, go fishing, travel to another village, and gather water for both bathing and cooking. The communal open-air bamboo terrace was often a playground for small children, dogs, and chickens, with pigs snorting below the elevated kitchens. To a middle-class boy from New Jersey, it was terribly exotic, the "real" Sarawak. Today virtually all of Sarawak's longhouses boast electricity and at least rudimentary plumbing. The fancy dress is reserved for religious festivals or when someone is paying them to stage a show. It's all very photogenic and exotic. But real life is pretty normal – the next day you're likely to meet a star dancer at the 7-Eleven or at the university lecture hall.

The folks at Serubah Ulu joined the tourist band-wagon for a while, but eventually the tour operators sought other destinations. I was given several reasons, take your pick: the longhouse people weren't sufficiently welcoming, the longhouse wasn't sufficiently "tradi-tional" (tourists were disturbed by the motorcycles and sacks of fertilizer kept on the communal porch), the longhouse folks raised their fees too high.

So, was I an interloper? A voyeur? A concerned

outsider who genuinely wanted to learn something from the people of Serubah Ulu? Or was I, god forbid, just another tourist?

Sometimes, especially at dinner parties, I might suggest that I visit isolated hill tribes in order to write gritty, empathetic exposés of environmental and social injustices and changing cultures, leaving unsaid but implied the suggestion that my prose is as smooth as old bourbon, as sinewy as cafeteria steak.

That's all true, but it's also a lot of politically correct hogwash. There is a lot of ego involved. I like to test myself physically, do things that my friends wouldn't, get off the beaten track to prove my credentials as a *serious traveler*. Does it matter that I'm not an academically inclined researcher or ethno-biologist? Perhaps a visit like mine, organized by Unding's daughter, is equally valid, a friend of the family, sort of, coming to pay a visit.

THE IBANS ARE AMONG THE MOST STUDIED TRIBAL groups by anthropologists, who have recorded Iban healing songs, their bird omens, their courtship rituals (premarital sex used to be no big deal), their social structure (pretty flat, and women have a strong voice), their architecture, their weaving, their animal spirit guides – whatever could generate a Ph.D. has been examined and footnoted.

I don't claim expertise in the rich assortment of Iban traditional deities and spirits. I know there's a supreme god, then seven medium-ranked gods, plus an abundance of mystical people, omens, and spirits. Complex rituals and chants, admonitions and augeries.

How pervasive are these modern realities in weakening the influence of people like Unding and his traditional beliefs?

The hint to the answer is that the traditional ways are referred to as *Pengarap Lama*, literally Old Belief. Ask any teenager. Old isn't cool.

I conducted a very informal, admittedly limited, and totally unscientific survey of Iban young people in Kuching and Sri Aman. I asked them two questions: How many of the major Iban bird omens can you name? And how many players in the English Premier League can you recall?

When given hints, they said they had heard of the bird omens but were hazy about what each one did. They were more at home discussing English football, and names like Wayne Rooney, Steven Gerrard, and Frank Lampard came without much prompting.

FOR MY INFORMAL SURVEY I CHOSE THE SEVEN IBAN OMEN birds for a reason. Although not the supreme symbols of Iban culture, they are messengers of the gods and regulate daily behavior. At least they did in earlier days. Today they are largely irrelevant in the modern *vie quotidienne*.

Nevertheless, they are the meat and potatoes of anthropologists because the interpretation of their blessings and warnings can be impenetrable to all but the most tenacious (and well-read) outsiders.

Consider just one example:

The *embuas*, a banded kingfisher – *Lacedo pulchella* – illustrates the complexity of Iban cosmology.

Like all kingfishers it is a beautiful bird; the male has a bright blue head and its wings and tail are distinctively striped in blue and white. It is often called the "mourning bird" but, like many such omens, it can indicate good or bad luck depending on the circumstances and the proclivities of the person doing the interpretation.

The analysis of Iban bird omens has long fascinated anthropologists because of their ambiguity. Seeing, or even hearing, the *embuas* can mean good luck or bad luck for activities as diverse as cockfighting (depends in part on whether you have already taken your bath in the river when you spot the bird), whether you are collecting rubber from the forest, whether you are more than halfway into your journey, whether the bird's call comes from the left or right, whether it is sighted near your chickens, whether you are visiting elders or children. And the message can be modified if the other six bird omens are present. There are more permutations of Iban bird omens than a grandmaster's chess moves. In one study, researcher Gregory Nyanggau Mawar highlighted the contradictory nature of *embuas*: "If it flies into your house and perches on you, it is not a good omen. It foretells that you will be distressed by the deaths of a number of very close relatives," Mawar wrote. "However, if you visit a sick person who is older than you, and you hear the voice of *embuas* after you have seen the roof of his house, it indicates that the sick person will be instantly cured after your visit."

This kind of cultural complexity cries out for a spiritual bard, a priest, someone who can interpret the signals of the gods. That person, in Iban, is a *lemambang*, who deals in ceremonies and mystical rituals.

The *manang* has a more pragmatic role. He (and often she) engages bad spirits and urges them to leave the body of his suffering patients. Call him a medicine man, or a healer, or a traditional doctor. He's all of those things. And his breed is dying out.

THE MOST STRIKING DECORATION IN THE MAIN ROOM of Unding's family's longhouse "room" is a commercially printed poster, about as big as a large bed sheet. It is the kind of canvas banner that middle-class Sarawakians have printed up in town for birthdays, anniversaries, business events. It reads "Selamat Ari-Jadi-90" (happy 90th-birthday), and features a large photo of a smiling and spry Unding, sporting a spiky crewcut and surrounded by a dozen colorful balloons and prominent images of Tweety Bird and the cute dog Lady (from *Lady and the Tramp*), both wearing conical party hats.

We'll have to accept the estimate of his age on faith, since, like others of his generation, Unding isn't sure when he was born. In the pre-literate days parents would recall that a child was born when the hill rice was grown in such-and-such a location, or when the Japanese soldiers came, or when there was a big fire and the longhouse had to be moved.

When the government decided that everyone should have an identity card, Unding's parents fudged on the boy's age. He was (probably) fifteen, but they told the official he was eighteen so he could get a passport. The official said "don't push your luck" and made him seventeen. Since the identity card was issued in December, that's the de facto month of his birth.

Why a passport? It relates to the *berjalai* that every able-bodied Iban young man undertakes. *Berjalai* can roughly be interpreted as a rite-of-passage journey, a leaving home to seek adventure and wealth and a first tattoo. In the old days a *berjalai* might result in the young man returning to the longhouse with an enemy's head. Today a young Iban man might work in a timber camp, or in the natural gas plant in Bintulu, or attend university. Today he might return with a flat screen TV or an engineering degree or a hard hat reading "Bechtel Saudi." Same game, different rewards. For his *berjalai* Unding went to neighboring Brunei and brought back a souvenir that hangs on his wall – a small tapestry showing the Ka'aba in Mecca. I asked him why he's hung that particular image, since he is not Muslim. "Just for the memory of the trip to [largely Muslim] Brunei," he said.

I WATCHED HIM AT WORK.

A family of four came to see Unding one evening. A woman, twenty-four but looking older, had been debilitated by severe migraine headaches since the birth of her last child a year earlier. She had been to see Western doctors and had spent almost $1,000 in consultations and treatments. Seeing the *manang* was her last hope.

Unding chats with the woman for a while and then covers himself with a *pua*, a woven blanket. He holds two *parangs* (machetes), claps them together, and gives a hooting call. A TV in the next room broadcasts a game show. He removes the *pua* and talks with the woman and her husband. It's all very social, with a fair bit of joking.

Unding rubs homemade medicated oil on her fore-head and unpacks his collection of amulets, bundled in a few tatty plastic bags. He rubs a stone he describes as Raja Genali (king of eels), which he found floating in the river following a dream he had, on the woman's temples. She takes off her shirt and he rubs her throat with a stone he claims is a meteorite. From a different bottle, which looks like it once contained cheap brandy, Unding rubs more oil on her back, legs, and stomach, all the while mumbling prayers. That's it, about five minutes of treatment. Unding's wife joins the group, serves sweet tea, and everybody has a good natter.

I later asked Unding what was wrong with the woman, who drove half an hour to Unding's longhouse. He explains that after giving birth, she didn't follow the traditional belief to keep her lower back warm and now is suffering because spirits entered her body. The clinging *parangs* helped him ask the spirits to tell him what action to take.

WHEN I ARRIVED AT THE LONGHOUSE I GAVE HIM GIFTS, much as in the West when you're invited to someone's house you bring a bottle of wine and a cheesecake.

Some fresh fish and vegetables from the Sri Aman market. Some tinned goods. Some biscuits for the kids. A bottle of whiskey – I knew Unding himself didn't drink much, but my guide Bayang explained that perhaps the alcohol could be brought out in the evening to lubricate a little longhouse party. And I gave him a rather nice amulet of Ganesha, the Hindu elephant god, thinking that he might be able to use it in his work. I explained its significance, told him it had been given to me by a Thai shaman, and made a case for its usefulness and universality.

He seemed underwhelmed by the Ganesha and instead showed me his own magic charms – a wild boar's tooth, a chunk of petrified wood, a potion made of snake venom and herbs.

I COLLECT PROTECTION CHARMS FOR OUR HOUSE IN Geneva, and I thought an Iban charm couldn't hurt.

Unding showed me some designs he had created (using white finger paint, it looked like) on the brown paper covers of school exercise books. He had a bunch of them, ready to go; obviously lots of people seek homeowner's insurance. I asked if I could buy one, expecting him to offer it to me, sort of quid pro quo for the

Ganesha. He asked for $15, which I gave him. I hung it in the entryway of my house in Geneva; since then we haven't been burgled, burned, or invaded by bad spirits.

DO SHAMANS CURE?
AND IF SO, HOW?

For a scientifically trained observer, it's difficult to write about tribal shamanism without letting a knowing snicker into the party. Incantations, amulets, odd and colorful vêtements, archaic languages, blood sacrifices, bizarre symbolism, and unshakable beliefs that strange rituals will generate the desired outcome permeate the topic.

That certainly describes shamanism; it also seems to describe most major religions.

The Western view is that illness is caused by physical complications – a nasty bacteria, a greedy virus, a worm or a blood clot or a fungus.

The alternative view, let's call it the traditional perception, is that illnesses can be caused by bad spirits. Western medicine can't always do the job, so a patient needs to call in a different type of healer.

Of course practitioners of Western medicine know well the positive effects of the placebo effect, in which an injection or tablet of a neutral substance (sugar is popular) can mimic the effects of a genuine pharmaceutical. In these cases it appears that the physician is imbued with shamanic-like powers; the patient believes the treatment will work, so it does.

And what about mental illness?

Is schizophrenia, for example, a physical problem with the brain's wiring? Or does it stem from a mischievous spirit subverting normal functions?

Are there such entities as spirits? Can energy have a positive or negative influence on our bodies? How can we account for spontaneous healing in people with incurable diseases? Why does laughter seem to encourage healing, just as having a hospital room with a view of trees speed post-surgery healing?

I don't know the answers to these questions.

I do, however, agree with philosopher and medical doctor Deepak Chopra that "the physical world, including our bodies, is a response of the observer. We create our bodies as we create the experience of the world." Put another way, as Hamlet said to Horatio: "There are more things in heaven and earth ... than are dreamt of in your philosophy." I like science. I believe in science, in cause and effect, in Newton's Three Laws. Yet I feel there are things out there that are beyond our ken, that the body works in strange ways, that we have only begun to understand the mind-body-spirit continuum. Within that continuum, is there room for a man like Unding? You tell me.

A victim of eco-genocide.

HEADHUNTERS FIGHT FOR CONTROL OF FORESTS

Ethnic massacre is one more bloody battle in the history of eco-conflicts.

SAMPIT, CENTRAL KALIMANTAN, INDONESIA

A friend sent a horrifying photo of an Asian girl, maybe six years old, lying on the ground, her arms splayed at impossible angles. Her dress is hiked up and her head is tilted from her body, like a broken puppet's. On closer examination I could see that her head had been sliced off, and not too carefully placed near her neck.

I will call this nameless girl Dewi. She was beheaded during the 2001 massacre of some five hundred immigrants from the arid island of Madura by gangs of the indigenous residents of Indonesian Borneo, collectively (if somewhat misleadingly) called Dayaks.

The killings were ethnic-specific – all of the victims were Madurese; the Dayak marauders, who had the support of their community leaders, left their Javanese and Balinese immigrant neighbors untouched.

What could spark such hostility?

One of the oft-ignored underlying triggers behind communal violence such as this is the fight for control of a people's natural resources.

John Walker, a lecturer in politics at University College, the Australian Defence Force Academy, says, "Far from having its origins in ethnicity, the present killings in Central Kalimantan, like those in western Kalimantan in 1998–99, reflect deep conflict over natural resources."

In the current Borneo scenario, the Indonesian government, building on Dutch policies of the 1930s, encouraged farmers from the overpopulated islands of Java, Bali, and Madura to "transmigrate" to lesser-populated outer islands, such as Borneo and New Guinea. The new settlers – there were some one hundred thousand Madurese in Kalimantan at the time of the massacres, many of whom have since left or been evacuated – were given traditional Dayak land and encouraged to cut down the forests and make farms. The Dayaks, who lived, to varying degrees, in some kind of harmony with nature, objected. But as Walker adds, "Indonesia does not guarantee indigenous people's rights over land." The Dayaks were left disenfranchised, land-poor, and angry.

Michael Dove, of Yale University, adds, "For three decades, the indigenous Dayak have seen their natural resource base steadily eroded. Vast amounts of Dayak lands and forests have been destroyed or appropriated for logging concessions, rubber and oil-palm plantations, pulp plantations, and transmigration sites."

Riska Orpa Sari, a Dayak woman who wrote *Riska: Memories of a Dayak Girlhood*, says the current conflict is based on control of the forests. "For centuries, our needs and rights have been denied by the government," she says.

"A flow of human beings has been sent like cattle to Kalimantan," Orpa Sari said. "Thousands of hectares of lush rainforest have been clear-cut to fill the need for land for the newcomers [and] the source of life for the Dayak and many rare species of wildlife [has been] intensively cut and timbered.

"So, betrayed and exploited, the anger exploded. Being used, neglected, and ignored left our people bitter. Vengeance emerged. The need to defend our land has come to the surface, the need to take our land and natural world back."

While recognizing that the cause of violent conflicts around the world are complex and involve economic, ethnic, racial, religious, and political arguments, the fight for control of nature has been one of the most important, but frequently overlooked root causes of bloody ethnic and political conflicts. Unfortunately, Kalimantan's eco-war is not an isolated case.

The conflict in Somalia, for example, is a war, in part, between clans who are fighting over access to grazing lands. In Mexico, the Zapatistas in Chiapas were fighting above all about who was going to decide how their resources were to be allocated. The numerous fights in the Congo focus on who has access to minerals. In the forests of Amazonia, tribes of Indians who not only take heads but also shrink them (at least historically) are continuing their battles against gold miners who are moving into their territories, often with the support of national military forces that do not appreciate cultural diversity.

IN 1998 I VISITED A GROUP OF DAYAKS IN A SETTLEMENT called Tanah Merah (Red Earth), upriver from Samarinda in Kalimantan. These are people from the Kenyah tribe, who have had no role in the Dayak-Madurese violence. Ironically, these people also were internal transmigrants, having been resettled several decades ago from their traditional homes further upriver. I stood on a hilltop with Pak Pajan, the village chief. I had just spent a few hours with him in old-growth forest, where the air was cool underneath the forest canopy and ripe with the scent of decay and rebirth – opposite forces that reflect Asian philosophy's desire to come to terms with polarities that define our existence. It was perhaps five degrees centigrade hotter outside the shelter of the forest, and the barren neighboring slopes, upon which would be planted agro-business monocultures of eucalyptus or acacia, seemed to stoically wither under the equatorial sun. Pajan's people, part of a tribe of some forty thousand and found mostly in Borneo's highlands, practice shifting cultivation and rely on the forest for food, shelter, and as the foundation of their cultural heritage. But the Kenyah were being smothered by land-hungry immigrants and government plantation schemes that wipe out rain forests. Pajan did not speak about wild rebellion, but clearly he was a troubled man, caught in a Borneo squeeze-play. I wondered what his flash point would be?

DEWI WAS CAUGHT IN A CROSSFIRE OF EMOTIONS.

On the one hand you had the Madurese, known to be aggressive and proud – Muslim folks who were interlopers in Borneo.

On the other hand you had Dayaks, similarly aggressive and proud, largely Christian with a strong underpinning of traditional beliefs, who had been in Borneo for centuries.

They both wanted the same bits of forest.

Dayak writer Riska Orpa Sari noted, "I know that the Dayak people want to live in peace with nature. We are the people of the forest. We do not make peace with people who destroy our home."

Dewi was a victim of that conflict.

The author, hungry and lost in Sulawesi,
testing his survival skills.

PASS ME A RAT, I'M A SURVIVOR

Does TV success depend on brawn or brain?

PULAU TIGA, SABAH, MALAYSIA

've just downloaded the form to be a Survivor. Surviving seems to be in the news these days and I want to become part of this evolutionary trend.

My ambition is to join the made-for-TV series *Survivor*. On the program screening now, sixteen people have volunteered to live on Pulau Tiga, an island off the Borneo coast of Sabah, East Malaysia. The last one to survive a series of votes by their colleagues stands to win a million dollars. As I write this, thirty-eight-year-old soccer mom Gretchen Cordy became the seventh castaway to be voted off the island, as the survivors shifted their objective from maintaining a strong group dynamic to saving their own skins.

In the early days of *Survivor* it was the elderly, weak, or annoying who were voted off, based on the logic that the two tribes needed strong, clever members who could throw a spear, row a canoe, catch a fish, or build a shelter.

But now, in the latter stages of the competition, people are voting off the ones most competent to survive.

"Of course I voted for her [to get kicked off the island]," contestant Richard Hatch, 39, said calmly after voting in the Tribal Council. "She was a threat to win."

"I consider it the highest compliment," Cordy, a former survival instructor for the U.S. Air Force explained. "People didn't vote me off because I was weak; they voted me off because I was strong."

Of course some survivors in the news these days don't have the option of escaping with a CBS-TV crew.

Not too far from Pulau Tiga, a multinational group of scuba-diving tourists were kidnapped from Sabah's Sipadan Island and hustled to the southern Philippines, where they have been held captive by a rebel Muslim group. No picnic for these folks. Barring any dramatic escapes, these people will only survive if external negotiators conclude a deal with the kidnappers.

SURVIVAL IS THE KEY TO EVOLUTION, AND BRITISH naturalist Alfred Russel Wallace developed his preliminary thoughts on evolution in 1855, while in Sarawak.

Wallace didn't understand the concept of genetics (Mendel only published his seminal paper eleven years later), but he intuitively knew that somehow an individual's traits get passed on to future generations.

Logically then, the best way to survive is not as an individual, but to transmit your genes onto healthy offspring.

THE *SURVIVOR* TV SHOW THAT I WANT TO JOIN, OF course, isn't about true survival. If these mostly young, mostly attractive, somewhat articulate Americans were really stranded, Robinson Crusoe-like, on a tropical island, the men might not worry about voting off a woman who is not adept at rat catching. A better long-term survival strategy, at least for a guy, might be to ensure that plenty of women of breeding age would remain on the island while eliminating male competitors (but perhaps keeping one strong, loyal, dumb guy around just in case the other tribe attacks).

Let's say I make it to the Australian Outback, where the next Survivor series will be filmed. What if my fellow survivors vote against me?

My ego would be hurt, for sure.

But at least I should be able to get another column out of the experience.

THE ULTIMATE OBJECTIVE OF SURVIVING, IN BIOLOGICAL terms, is to pass on your genes. The good news is that some women consider writers sexy. Go figure.

So that's my primary strategy. I'm nearsighted, have a wonky knee and a stiff back, and could never finish a triathlon. But, luckily for me, a sense of humor, self-confidence, and the ability to make an after-dinner toast are attractive qualities to some women.

SOME TRIBESMEN, NOTABLY THE PENANS, CAN SURVIVE in the gloom and damp of the Borneo rainforest.

Westerners have a much tougher time, and people a lot stronger than I am have struggled to survive even a few weeks in the rainforest.

How would I fare on the American reality-TV series *Naked and Afraid*? In this program, a man and woman who have never met are marooned in a hostile natural environment, with just two tools (most couples choose a cooking pot and a machete), without fire, without food, without water, and without clothes. They have to survive for three weeks.

For an episode titled "Breaking Borneo," broadcast in 2013, the two contestants had infinitely more survival skills than I possess.

Julie Wright, 30, is a wilderness instructor, skilled in tanning hides, "primitive fire," plant identification, and "staying hidden." She's a tall, robust woman who makes her own buckskin skirts and moccasins.

Puma Cabra, 38, describes himself as a tattoo artist. He is short and wiry, with a chin beard and long, Tarzan-like hair. He recalls how his family ran a chop-shop garage until his uncle was murdered by a bike gang. He enjoys living in the forest with "nothing but his knife and his knowledge." He has faced mountain lions and pulled himself out of six avalanches.

Neither had ever been in a rainforest (which they called "jungle").

Of course these folks weren't alone. There was always a film crew watching over them, they wore small microphones that were hidden in necklaces that looked like homemade rawhide and bone jewelry (the batteries are kept in a "natural looking" woven pouch, according to Borneo-based film producer Edgar Ong, who worked on the program).

Neither participant made it to the end. Puma drank some bad water, suffered a high fever, and quit early; Julie dropped out a few days later.

Captivating television, perhaps. But I marvel at the gullibility of the audience to think they're watching a real life-or-death situation. After all, Julie and Puma were followed almost 24/7 by a camera crew, and the production team stayed not too far away in a camp that included communications, transport, medical care, and food. Contestants might go crazy, but it's unlikely they would die.

Me? I would probably get real hungry, real cold, real depressed, real quickly. But then you never know how people will react under pressure.

WILL I MAKE IT AS A SURVIVOR? FAT CHANCE. I JUST re-read the *Survivor* application form. "You must be a United States citizen and live in the United States."

I live in Switzerland.

So this is what it's come down to — survival means first meeting bureaucratic requirements. I'm going to grill a rat, write a sonnet, and rethink my strategy.

Ali, in an 1862 photo taken in Singapore.

From: *The Malay Archipelago*, Alfred Russel Wallace, 1869.

THE SEARCH FOR ALI

Borneo lad takes part in momentous discovery,
then totally ignored.

KUCHING, SARAWAK

he Borneo newspapers in 1858 sported a large headline: "Local Borneo lad helps develop theory of evolution."

The Borneo-based reporters told how a teenaged cook from Sarawak named Ali assisted Alfred Russel Wallace on his eight-year adventure in Southeast Asia, culminating in Wallace's development of the Theory of Natural Selection.

The Borneo newspapers revealed how Ali nursed Wallace during a malarial fit, giving the older Englishman strength and moral support to write the theory that changed the way we view ourselves and our place in the scheme of things.

The Borneo newspapers, of course, said none of these things. Ali was then, and remained, a footnote, a historical afterthought written in small type.

I HAVE SPENT FORTY YEARS TRYING TO FIND OUT MORE about Ali. Who he was, why he went with Wallace, and where he ultimately settled. It's been a lonely quest.

WESTERN HISTORY TREATS FAMOUS EXPLORERS AS individuals who braved the elements alone, stoic, unflappable, and with immense strength of character and fortitude. But actually, all explorers, the great as well as the overlooked, rely on often-unheralded people to assist in their odyssey. Lewis and Clark had Sacagawea, Edmund Hillary had Tenzing Norgay. Ferdinand Magellan had Enrique, a slave he bought in Malacca and encouraged (I use the term advisedly) to renounce Islam and convert to Catholicism. Enrique became Magellan's interpreter, guide, and friend; he is also possibly the first person to complete the circumnavigation of the globe, since Magellan was killed in the Philippines before finishing the epic journey while Enrique continued the voyage.

British naturalist and explorer Alfred Russel Wallace had Ali, and without Ali's assistance it is unlikely Wallace would have been as successful as he was.

That's about all we know.

ALFRED RUSSEL WALLACE HAD ONLY BEEN IN THE Malay Archipelago for six months when he went to Sarawak, at the invitation of James Brooke, the famed "White Rajah" of Borneo.

Wallace was enthusiastic and full of energy. During his eighteen months in Sarawak, Wallace collected two thousand "distinct kinds" of beetles; during one two-week period he was averaging twenty-four *new* beetle species every day. In one twenty-six-night stretch he collected 1,386 moths. He shot and pickled seventeen orangutans.

But he was new to Southeast Asia. He spoke just a few words of Malay, the lingua franca of the region. He was an innocent abroad.

Here's how Wallace described his engagement of Ali as personal assistant:

> When I was at Sarawak in 1855 I engaged a Malay boy named Ali as a personal servant, and also to help me to learn the Malay language by the necessity of constant communication with him. He was attentive and clean, and could cook very well.

THERE'S AN AWFUL LOT WE DON'T KNOW ABOUT ALI. For a start, we have no idea of his patronym. No family connections have been unearthed. We don't know where he came from. Did he come from Sarawak, where he was first employed? Or perhaps he came from further afield: The Earl of Cranbrook and Adrian G. Marshall, writing in the Sarawak Museum Journal, speculate that "it is probable that Ali was in fact a roving youth of Malay race born and raised outside Sarawak." They note that the one time Wallace quotes Ali the lad:

addressed [Wallace] in the Bazaar Malay typical of the area of Dutch control ... Ali's language, his skills and his self-confident authority are wholly inconsistent with the image of an unsophisticated Sarawak lad ... and Ali's prowess as a boatman could have been gained through serving on inter-island voyages.

Other questions persist. Did Ali have family in Sarawak? How well was he educated, and did he speak a bit of English? And most interestingly for me, what did Ali think of the gangly, bearded Englishman who spent his days collecting innumerable insects and his nights writing, by the light of an oil lamp, in a small notebook?

WE DON'T KNOW UNDER WHAT CIRCUMSTANCES Wallace engaged Ali, but here's my theory.

I figure that James Brooke saw how hapless Wallace was, took him aside, and said, "Look here Wallace, here in Sarawak people know you're my friend and they will tolerate your curious behavior and listen to your baby-talk-Malay and won't cheat you *too* much. But out there [no doubt he was pointing south to the maze of countless Indonesian islands where Wallace was heading] they're going to eat you alive." Brooke then asked one of his Malay assistants if he had a young relative who would be willing to go off on an adventure from which he might not return. The result was the Ali-Wallace partnership.

I DON'T WANT TO OVERSTATE HIS INVOLVEMENT, BUT Ali was present when Wallace developed the first step in his quest to understand and prove evolution.

It was the rainy season in early 1855 and Wallace was staying in James Brooke's cottage in Santubong, about half an hour from Sarawak's current capital of Kuching.

Ali kept Wallace's spirits up by cooking for him and teaching him Malay.

It was too wet for serious collecting, so Wallace had ample time to ponder the question of how species evolve. During these soggy months Wallace wrote what became known as the Sarawak Law, a first step toward his Theory of Natural Selection, which he developed in 1858 while in Ternate, eastern Indonesia.

To summarize, the Sarawak Law said: "Every species has come into existence coincident both in space and time with a pre-existing closely allied species."

That's it. New species are linked to previous species. They didn't just fall out of the sky, or appear at the whim of a Do-It-Yourself-Inclined God.

WALLACE DESCRIBED HOW ALI GREW INTO THE JOB AS they roamed through the isolated islands of Indonesia:

> He soon learnt to shoot birds, to skin them properly, and latterly even to put up the skins very neatly. Of course he was a good boatman, as are all Malays, and in all the difficulties or dangers of our journeys he was quite undisturbed and ready to do anything required of

him. He accompanied me through all my travels, sometimes alone, but more frequently with several others, and was then very useful in teaching them their duties, as he soon became well acquainted with my wants and habits.

In eastern Indonesia Ali was responsible for collecting a bird that became one of Wallace's treasures:

Just as I got home I overtook Ali returning from shooting with some birds hanging from his belt. He seemed much pleased, and said, "Look here, sir, what a curious bird!" holding out what at first completely puzzled me. I saw a bird with a mass of splendid green feathers on its breast, elongated into two glittering tufts; but what I could not understand was a pair of long white feathers, which stuck straight out from each shoulder. Ali assured me that the bird stuck them out this way itself when fluttering its wings, and that they had remained so without his touching them. I now saw that I had got a great prize, no less than a completely new form of the bird of paradise ... This striking novelty has been named by Mr. G.R. Gray, of the British Museum, *Semioptera Wallacei* [today *Semioptera wallacii*], or "Wallace's Standard-wing."

And eventually Wallace described Ali as "my head man":

Ali, the Malay boy whom I had picked up in Borneo, was my head man. He had already been with me a year, could turn his hand to any thing, and was quite attentive and trustworthy. He was a good shot, and fond of shooting, and I had taught him to skin birds very well.

Wallace was traveling independently – he had no government or military support system. He also had little cash – he was a self-described "beetle collector" who earned enough to survive by sending natural history specimens to his beetle agent in London, who then sold the critters to enthusiastic collectors. (Charles Darwin, on the other hand, during his famous five-year voyage on the HMS Beagle, lived on-board in what was, in effect, a floating base camp, with Royal Navy sailors on hand to provide security, logistics, laundry, and food. He had a permanent, dry place to write his notes and mount his specimens. It provided Darwin with all the adventure he wanted; he never again left England.)

Wallace moved camp some one hundred times during his eight years in Southeast Asia, and we can imagine that greedy local merchants saw big profits when a white man like Wallace came along to buy supplies. Ali probably reduced the amount that Wallace was overcharged, helping in negotiations with self-important village chiefs: *Hello, good sir, do you mind if I set up a camp in your forest and shoot your birds and collect your butterflies?* Ali organized porters and laborers; he administered the thousands of annoying details of travel.

CHRISTOPHER VOGLER IS A HOLLYWOOD SCREENWRITER whose book *The Writer's Journey* explores how a classical mythic structure is used in popular films such as *Casablanca*, *The Wizard of Oz*, *Star Wars*, and *Close Encounters of the Third Kind.* "All stories consist of a few common structural elements found universally in myths, fairy tales, dreams, and movies," Vogler says. "They are known collectively as The Hero's Journey."

One essential archetype in the hero's journey is the character Vogler calls the Mentor (and which philosopher Joseph Campbell refers to as Wise Old Man or Wise Old Woman), who teaches and protects heroes and gives them gifts. In classical mythology as well as contemporary novels, the Mentor is a sage adult – Merlin guiding King Arthur, the Fairy Godmother helping Cinderella, or a veteran sergeant giving advice to a rookie cop.

If you wish to plot Ali's hero's journey in this way, then Wallace was clearly the Mentor, and Ali took the role of a keen, but initially naïve, son, who grows in competence and confidence as the story progresses. We can assume that when Wallace met Ali, the Malay teenager had never left Sarawak, probably had never had a conversation with a European, and had a limited worldview. Wallace took him on a magnificent journey lasting almost eight years, and by the time Ali and Wallace parted company, Ali no doubt had grown considerably.

"Ali would have been one of the most widely traveled Malays of his age," according to Jerry Drawhorn of California State University, Sacramento. "He would have seen most of what is today modern Indonesia (Papua to Sumatra). He would have seen the ancient Hindu temples of Java; the modern metropolises of Batavia and Singapore; the primitive villages of the people of Dorey;

and the stylized royal courts of central Java. He tasted modern science and medicine and yet retained his beliefs in ghosts and men who could transform into tigers."

WALLACE HAD TWO BASE CAMPS, SINGAPORE AND Ternate – places where he could keep books, supplies and specimens, where he could have a good wash and eat decent food, and where he could recuperate from his difficult travels.

The most important of the two was Ternate, an island of picture-postcard beauty to the east of Sulawesi, famous as one of the sources of cloves, a spice that triggered the European colonial epoch.

Wallace's time in Ternate was peaceful and restorative, where he could "return to after my voyages to the various islands of the Moluccas and New Guinea, where I could pack my collections, recruit my health, and make preparations for future journeys."

This is where Wallace had what might be the most famous malaria fit of all time. Most people have nightmares about demons, flights of fancy, and great adventures; Wallace's breakthrough dream starred Thomas Robert Malthus:

> I was suffering from a sharp attack of intermittent fever, and every day during the cold and succeeding hot fits had to lie down for several hours, during which time I had nothing to do but to think over any subjects

then particularly interesting me. One day something brought to my recollection Malthus's "Principles of Population," ["An Essay on the Principle of Population"] which I had read twelve years before. I thought of his clear exposition of "the positive checks to increase" – disease, accidents, war, and famine – which keep down the population of savage races to so much lower an average than that of more civilized peoples. It then occurred to me that these causes or their equivalents are continually acting in the case of animals also; and as animals usually breed much more rapidly than does mankind, the destruction every year from these causes must be enormous in order to keep down the numbers of each species, since they evidently do not increase regularly from year to year, as otherwise the world would long ago have been densely crowded with those that breed most quickly. Vaguely thinking over the enormous and constant destruction which this implied, it occurred to me to ask the question, Why do some die and some live? And the answer was clearly, that on the whole the best fitted live. From the effects of disease the most healthy escape; from enemies, the strongest, the swiftest, or the most cunning ... Then it suddenly flashed upon me that this self-acting process would necessarily improve the race, because in every generation the inferior would inevitably be killed off and the superior would remain – that is, *the fittest would survive* ... I waited anxiously for the termination of my fit so that I might at once make notes for a paper on the subject [italics Wallace].

This, as they say, is eureka-time. Archimedes in his bath, Newton under the apple tree. Wallace in a cold sweat.

Wallace was keen to write his paper. Ali nursed him

through the debilitating illness. Once Wallace got back his strength, he got to work and wrote the paper over the next two evenings.

Wallace recognized what a significant breakthrough this was, and described his Ternate Paper as "the long-sought-for law of nature that solved the problem of the origin of species."

Wallace sent the paper to Charles Darwin.

Darwin, on receiving Wallace's "Ternate Paper," wrote to his friend, the noted geologist Charles Lyell: "I never saw a more striking coincidence; if Wallace had had my manuscript sketch, written out in 1842, he could not have made a better short abstract of it."

Thus began one of the most curious episodes in the history of science. Who had the idea first, Wallace or Darwin? Who got the credit, who deserves the credit? This isn't the place for that discussion; I cover it in *An Inordinate Fondness for Beetles*.

AFTER SEVEN YEARS TRAVELING THROUGHOUT THE Indonesian archipelago, Wallace and Ali made their way to Singapore. Wallace was getting on a ship to return to England. He was generous to the young man, still in his early twenties:

> On parting, besides a present in money, I gave [Ali] my two double-barrelled guns and whatever ammunition I had, with a lot of surplus stores ... which made him quite rich. He here, for the first time, adopted

European clothes, which did not suit him nearly so well as his native dress, and thus clad a friend took a very good photograph of him. I therefore now present his likeness to my readers as that of the best native servant I ever had, and the faithful companion of almost all my journeyings among the islands of the far East.

The photo to which Wallace refers shows a full-mouthed, dark-complexioned lad with wavy hair, thick eyebrows and broad nose, dressed in a dark European-style jacket and under-jacket, white shirt, and a white bow tie.

THEN WHAT? WHERE DID ALI GO?

Did Ali return to Kuching, the city of his birth, where he perhaps had relatives?

Perhaps he stayed in Singapore, a city he knew reasonably well and had a large Malay community.

Or did Ali return to Ternate, where he and Wallace had resided for many years?

In Sarawak today, people have a modest awareness of Wallace, and almost zero awareness of Ali. Among the few people who care about the Ali saga is Tom McLaughlin, an American historian and longtime Kuching resident.

McLaughlin believes that Ali returned to Kuching, and he bases his argument on the importance of *adat*, or custom, in which an adventuring young man has both an obligation as well as a desire to return to the village of his birth.

McLaughlin theorizes that Ali was from the Minang-kabau ethnic group in Sumatra, a matriarchal society where boys were encouraged to leave home to study at the local surau or mosque. Kuching had (and has) a well-established surau just a few hundred meters from James Brooke's palace; then and now they taught young men religion as well as languages and domestic skills like sewing and cooking.

McLaughlin has spoken about Ali with various Sarawak historical societies and Malay cultural organizations. No one in those groups had much interest in the subject.

McLaughlin and his wife Suriani have visited all of the Malay villages around Kuching, hoping that some elder would remember the story about a great-great granduncle Ali.

They endured hours of small talk, endless politely offered cups of sweet tea and little flavorless pink cookies. They got no leads at all. McLaughlin did, however, find tax records from 1859 that indicated that a man named Ali had bought three houses. I pointed out that Ali was with Wallace in eastern Indonesia during that period, but McLaughlin suggests that Ali might have taken a sabbatical and returned to Kuching for several months. Given the nature of Ali's employment with Wallace, his lack of cash, the difficulty of making such a journey, and the commonness of the name Ali, I find McLaughlin's theory unconvincing.

PERHAPS ALI STAYED IN SINGAPORE? I PUT THE question to various Malay historians in Singapore and was greeted with polite interest and zero desire to follow up.

THAT LEAVES TERNATE, THE TOWN WHERE WALLACE had his eastern Indonesia base camp for some three and a half years.

This seems the most likely; indeed, Wallace refers to Ali's having established a family in Ternate:

> During our residence at Ternate he married, but his wife lived with her family, and it made no difference in his accompanying me whenever I went till we reached Singapore on my way home.

There are two morsels of evidence that Ali settled in Ternate after saying good-bye to Wallace in Singapore.

The first Ternate clue is provided by Tom McLaughlin, whose experience in Ternate undercuts his belief that Ali returned to Sarawak.

Traveling with his wife, McLaughlin visited a Muslim cemetery in Ternate. Aware it was a long shot, McLaughlin approached some women who were collecting aromatic flowers that had been scattered on the graves, and asked whether they knew of a grave for "Ali Wallace." They took McLaughlin through a warren of small paths to a grave that had been newly renovated with blue and white kitchen tiles. They explained that just two weeks earlier, two "Malays" from Jakarta and a "white man" had visited the site, paid for the improvements, and said some prayers. Malay graves are not marked with the name of the deceased and there is no way to confirm that it is indeed Ali who is buried there.

The only way to confirm that the body in the newly improved grave is that of Ali would be to exhume it and conduct a cranial and facial reconstruction from the skull, similar to the stereolithography process used to create a portrait of England's Richard III after his body was found in a parking lot in Leicester, England. Anthropological artists might then compare the face of the purported adult Ali with the only existing photo of Ali as a young man, to see whether there are similarities. If it is believed that the skull is that of Ali, then DNA from the skeleton could be taken and compared with the DNA of current-day residents of Ternate and neighboring islands to see if any relatives might be found. I consider the possibility of such an exhumation and scientific analysis unlikely.

However, there is another, more convincing stream of evidence that Ali settled in Ternate.

In 1907 American naturalist Thomas Barbour visited Ternate and claimed he met Ali, who was by then an old man. In his autobiography of 1943 Barbour wrote:

Here came a real thrill, for I was stopped in the street [in Ternate] one day as my wife and I were preparing to climb up to the Crater Lake. With us were Ah Woo with his butterfly net, Indit and Bandoung, our well-trained Javanese collectors, with shotguns, cloth bags, and a vasculum for carrying the birds. We were stopped by a wizened old Malay man [he would have been around 52]. I can see him now, with a faded blue fez on his head. He said, 'I am Ali Wallace.' I knew at once that there stood before me Wallace's faithful companion of many years, the boy who not only helped him collect but nursed him when he was sick. We took his photograph and sent it to Wallace when we got home. He wrote me a delightful letter acknowledging it and reminiscing over the time when Ali had saved his life, nursing him through a terrific attack of malaria. This letter I have managed to lose, to my eternal chagrin.

There is no record of Barbour's original letter to Wallace, nor Wallace's letter in response.

Barbour mentioned Ali two other times. In the first he recalls asking Ali whether he had ever come across a lizard similar to the one collected by Barbour on a neighboring island. And in 1921 Barbour mentions his encounter with Ali in more detail and notes Ali had accompanied Wallace on "many a hazardous journey."

I WENT TO TERNATE AND SPOKE TO THE MAYOR AND various officials. I suggested they could place an article in the local paper; I even volunteered to write it. "Let's show his photo and story to the village elders," I suggested. "Let's get a university student to write a thesis on the search for Ali." I pointed out that this search could generate national, even international, news and be a stimulus for the tourist business. It would certainly help build local pride, which is always a good thing for elected officials to bask in. *Bagus*, everyone said. Good idea. Lots of enthusiasm, no action. Indonesian inertia? A dearth of intellectual curiosity? A reluctance to pursue a "foreign" idea?

In a fit of frustration, I went on what I knew would be a Quixotic quest. Surely, I thought, someone would have a memory of great-great granduncle Ali.

With the help of a friend who spoke the local dialect, I strolled through the Malay kampong, showed the photo to every old person I met, and asked if they had heard of this guy Ali.

I gave lectures to history students at universities in Ternate and neighboring cities and encouraged them to seek Ali. A few students I spoke with privately expressed polite interest, but they quickly zoned out when I explained that for their research they would have to speak with old folks in the villages and go through dusty records. "But that sounds like ... field work!" they would exclaim, before politely excusing themselves.

IT SEEMS AS IF ALI IS DESTINED TO REMAIN AN ENIGMA, a lost soul in the large filing cabinet labeled: People Who Did Important Things but Never Got Any Credit. I suspect we all have a bunch of Alis in our memory banks, folks who have helped us in innumerable ways, folks to whom we rarely raise a glass. We don't know Ali's birthday. But perhaps we might declare January 8, Wallace's birthday, as Global Ali Day, to give remembrance to those who nursed us, did us unexpected favors, who, sometimes, without our awareness, eased our paths.

Dewi, channeling Farida: "Meester, I'm coming for you."

"ARE YOU STRONG ENOUGH TO GO THROUGH WITH THIS?"

*Encounters with female vampire ghosts in
a city built on a ghost story.*

PONTIANAK, WEST KALIMANTAN, INDONESIA

" The shaman asks me a third time. "Are you sure you want to do this?"

I feel like I was back in high school again and my soccer coach, Charlie Koch, was looking down the bench to see who he could put into the game. Put me in, coach. I can do it. I'm ready.

The shaman was responding to a request I had made hours earlier. I was the first European to pose this particular challenge to the middle-aged man and he was checking my desire and commitment, and, I suppose, my strength to handle what might take place if he was successful.

Send me in, coach.

For the third time he offers me an easy out. He points to a thirty-something woman named Dewi, who was seated nearby, watching quietly.

"She's a medium. She can channel the spirit and you can watch. It'll be easier for you."

But I had come this far and can be stubborn when faced with a challenge.

Put me in, coach. I'm sure. I want to meet a pontianak.

IN THE INTER-WORLD, IN THE TWILIGHT MIST OF GRAY rainbows, hovering between dusk and dawn, joy and sorrow, life and death, dwell the ghosts. Wisps of smoke, certainly, but all too real for those who believe.

And the best place in the world to look for ghosts is the western tip of Borneo.

Not just any kind of ghost, but a very specific type of spirit that gives this city its name: Pontianak. The only city in the world named after a female vampire spirit who is eternally angry at men.

I am in Pontianak. I have visited various shamans over the previous few days and have heard a bunch of pontianak *stories. Now I want to "see" one for myself.*

A friend found a shaman who was willing to hold a séance and, through a medium, introduce me to a "real" pontianak. *The only hitch was that the shaman-for-hire had to pay the medium, buy offerings, cover his costs. "How much?" I asked. "About $650," my friend said.*

Time for Plan B.

ACCORDING TO LEGENDS, AND THERE ARE MANY, A *pontianak* is a misandrist for good reason: she is the spirit of a woman who died in childbirth, alone, abandoned by the child's father.

The word *pontianak* may be a corruption of the Malay *perempuan mati beranak* or "young woman who died in childbirth."

She preys on men, indiscriminately. She is pale, dressed in white, and horribly ugly, except when she's beautiful. You can only make a hideous ghost beautiful by hammering a nail into the hole on the nape of her neck; the spirit will then become an attractive and dutiful wife.

An alternative to the expensive séance was provided by my friend Din Osman, a local historian. One rainy afternoon we visited the home of one of his office colleagues, Rustammy. He runs a music café that is attached to his house, and in his home office I noticed a few electric guitars lying about, like a poor man's Hard Rock Café.

Rustammy explained the two options. I could "call" a pontianak *myself and have a one-on-one experience with her. Or I could "speak" with a* pontianak via *Dewi, who was quietly watching our discussion.*

We could do it that evening.

"Are you really strong enough?"

Send me in, coach.

A NOTE ON NOMENCLATURE (APOLOGIES, THIS GETS A bit confusing). In the Malay language, used in Malaysia, Singapore, Brunei, and parts of Indonesia, the term for this particular spirit is *pontianak*. In the closely related Indonesian language (the difference between the two languages might be compared to the difference between American English and Australian English), the term is *kuntilanak*. Even though the town of Pontianak is in Indonesia, they use the Malay word, *pontianak*, for their city and the Indonesian term, *kuntilanak*, for the ghost. For simplicity I will refer to the ghost as *pontianak*, regardless of whether it appears in Malaysia or Indonesia.

Also, the Malay term for a shaman/medicine man/ magician/healer is *bomoh*, while the Indonesian term is *dukun*.

When we get to Rustammy's house, there are ten people hanging around. Two additional men stroll in.

"Who are you?" Rustammy asks.

"We heard you were going to call a pontianak and we came over," the strangers say.

Rustammy is plussed. "I don't know you," he says to the men, angry, but in a polite Indonesian way. "How did you find out about this? Please leave."

I MET THE TENTH SULTAN OF PONTIANAK DURING A 2014 visit.

I was having dinner with two friends who are related to the royal family.

Over the grilled prawns and fish soup, one of my friends, a cousin of the sultan, said, "You're asking so many questions about the royal family, do you want to meet the sultan?"

"But it's already eight-thirty. Isn't it too late?"

"No problem."

So we forgot about dessert, walked to the riverbank, and boarded a comfortable wide-beamed boat that was a semi-permanent café. My friend asked the other patrons if they minded a little river cruise, I forked over a few dollars, and the boat was untied from the mooring. We chugged across the river to the sultan's *kraton* (palace) to meet Syarif Toto Thaha Alkadrie, the tenth sultan, the successor to a man who was Pontianak's first ghostbuster.

In 1771 a prince named Syarif Abdul Rahman al-Gadri, burdened with a dodgy reputation among seafarers and hassled by a vicious ongoing family feud at home, wanted to have a new start to his life. He sailed along the west Borneo coast and anchored near an empty stretch of land seventeen kilometers from the sea where two major rivers meet. It was a strategic place for a settlement, but it had been left empty because it was a swampy jungle believed to be a place of bad spirits – the *pontianaks*.

Local historian Din Osman recounted one of many tales of the founding of Pontianak. He said that for three days and three nights, the ghosts mocked the intruders, making an eerie "hee-hee-hee" laughing sound that infuriated Abdul Rahman.

Legend has it Abdul Rahman scared the *pontianaks* away in the same way he fought his earthly enemies, with a large bombardment of cannons. History is not an exact science here; myth and fact are joined at the hip. Some legends say that the spirits fled. Other myths say that the sultan never got rid of all the ghosts and was haunted for the remainder of his life.

Either way, Abdul Rahman became the first Sultan of Pontianak, and the town was given the name it has to this day. Every October 23, on the anniversary of the founding of the city, the local tourist office celebrates the event with a (redundantly named) Pontianak ghost festival.

THE BUSY TOWN OF PONTIANAK HAS SIX HUNDRED thousand people, a large university, shopping malls, traffic jams, and luxury hotels.

But the ghosts remain. Pontianak probably has more ghosts per capita than any other small city, and virtually everyone I spoke with has a ghost story to tell. It doesn't take long before I imagine the entire town bursting into song, like an Indonesian Busby Berkeley musical – "ooh-eee ... one-eyed, one-horned, flyin' purple people eater."

They're everywhere, and I challenge a visitor to find a citizen of the town who *doesn't* have a *pontianak* story.

Ghosts, sprites, demons, and things that go bump in

the night are rampant. They're in the banana trees. In cell phone towers, in dreams and, most definitely, in schools. And in the soup (don't eat at Auntie Aminah's, she might put a spell on you). There is a particularly nasty *pontianak* in the old house near the cemetery, where my sister-in-law's ex-boyfriend's motorcycle mechanic's grandfather was killed; just before he died he ran gibbering into the yard shouting, "I'm not the one who killed your baby, go back to your own world."

Din Osman's story is typical. In 1984 he was riding a motorcycle on the bridge over the Kapuas River, near the swampy site where the first sultan encountered the ghosts. On one end the bridge connected with a cemetery. Osman saw a *pontianak* walking across the span carrying a gravestone. He watched her for a while, then decided that safety was better than curiosity and sped away.

Many of the folks I spoke with speculated that the ghosts are spirits of dead women who are stuck between earth and heaven. "So you believe it," I would prod. "Not really," they would reply. "I don't believe in ghosts. But I saw it. I can't explain it. If it's not a ghost then what is it?"

WHAT IS IT? THE *PONTIANAK* CONUNDRUM IS TO LOGICAL reasoning as Fermat's Last Theorem is to mathematics. It *might* be true, but no one (and many wise people have tried) has proven it by using any of our recognizable proof procedures. People simply say, *I can't prove it. But I know that it is true.* What would Descartes have to say about that?

Rustammy explains what I must do and what I might expect. Suddenly, one of Rustammy's friends, a man named Andi, starts shouting. His eyes bulge, then he arches his back and pounds the table. "He's a foreigner," the man yells, looking in my direction. "It's not right."

"Ah, that's Datuk Jangut *[the Bearded Lord]," Rustammy says. "Andi goes into a trance easily. There are so many spirits in this room and some of them don't want to be bothered. Can you feel them?"*

No, I don't feel them. I have attended dozens of séances throughout Indonesia and other parts of Southeast Asia. I've seen men in trances speaking in tongues. Men in trances stabbing themselves with knives and broken glass. Men in trances claiming to be my father. One time a man in a trance said he was Moses and that he wanted me to go to the Middle East to stop the never-ending feud between the Israelis and the Palestinians.

Rustammy calmly tells the spirit that we aren't going to bother anybody, to just settle down and be cool. Datuk Jangut *leaves Andi's body without another word.*

WE FEAR THE UNKNOWN. WE SEEK TO UNDERSTAND the inexplicable, the implausible. *Pontianaks* are the taunting downside of religions – when you agree to follow a belief you drink the Kool-Aid of the proposition on offer: "Believe in my myths and rules and rituals and you'll be rewarded in the next life. No guarantee, of course. Trust me."

The metaphysical explanation is that when you die, the physical body returns to compost, while the soul flutters for eternity – maybe in heaven, maybe in hell.

However in death, as in nuclear power station engineering and unprotected sex, things can go disturbingly wrong. A soul gets waylaid, by accident or Cosmic Intention, who can pretend to know? And that soul wanders in a netherworld, like a blindfolded man playing pin the tail on the donkey long after the other party-goers, and the donkey itself, have gone home.

When an AirAsia flight from Surabaya to Singapore disappeared in late 2014, Jakarta Governor Basuki "Ahok" Tjahaja Purnama referred to the high density of ghosts and mystical phenomena in the region of Kalimantan, where the plane was last heard from. He joked that *jinn* (supernatural creatures in Islamic mythology and origin of the English genie) might be responsible for the disappearance of the plane. His statement was poorly received.

Too many people. Four of us go into an adjacent room, partly enclosed.

"You're really sure you are strong enough to see a pontianak?"

Yes, coach.

"Sit in a lotus position, close your eyes, and call the pontianak," Rustammy instructs.

I'm not comfortable sitting in a lotus position and sit against a wall instead.

"Hold your hands out in front of you."

Which I do.

"Close your eyes."

Which I do.

"Now call the pontianak."

Which I do. Do I need to say it out loud or to myself? I opt for a silent murmur. Hello, Ibu Pontianak! Good day to you. Miz Pontianak, where are you? I know you're here. Come to me. I want to see you.

"She's close, I can feel she's close," Rustammy says.

"Order her to come."

Get your vampire ass over here right now.

"She's right here," Rustammy insists. "I can feel her."

I don't feel her.

"Order her to come," Rustammy says, insistent that his tactics will work.

I'm not sure it's a good idea to boss around a female vampire ghost who hates men.

I mix the strategies of command and request.

Come closer, Madam Pontianak. Close to me, close to you. I order you. I command you. You're close. I want to see you.

And then my monkey-mind kicks in. I start to hum the Carpenters' song "Close to You." Why do birds suddenly appear, every time, you are near?

I want to giggle.

Do pontianaks *have a sense of humor? Do they appreciate music of the seventies?*

After about five additional minutes of unanswered entreaties and scraps of banal music I open my eyes. "Nothing," I say.

THE DISCIPLINE OF GHOST TAXONOMY IS STILL IN ITS infancy, and the spiritual world could certainly use someone like Swedish botanist Carl Linnaeus, who was to biological taxonomy what Brigitte Bardot was to the bikini.

One might argue that nature (and the spirit world), by definition, is chaotic and disorderly. But Linnaeus, who liked to say "God created, Linnaeus organized," strove for structure and logic; he was frustrated by the chaos in which mushrooms were mushrooms. Some were tasty, some were hallucinogenic, and some would kill you. True, they were all mushrooms, but not alike. Same-same but different. In the early eighteenth century Linnaeus lamented that there was no common, easy-to-use, universal system of nomenclature for different species, citing the case of the common tomato, which was described as *Solanum caule inermi herbaceo, foliis pinnatis incises* – the solanum with the smooth stem that is herbaceous and has incised pinnate leaves.

Ghost taxonomy is similarly chaotic and imprecise.

In *The Malaysian Book of the Undead*, researcher Danny

Lim catalogues one hundred twenty-six different types of ghosts, vampires, *hantus*, demons, were-tigers, evil spirits, goblins, and other creatures you don't want to meet on a dark and stormy night. Malaysia has plenty of faults, but you gotta love a nation with enough ghosts for more than ten football teams.

Like a taxonomist, Lim suggests various classifications.

There are the "class of disease-causing ghosts" like *hantu cika*, which causes colic, or *hantu sawan*, which causes convulsions (*sawan*) in young children.

He names nature spirits that inhabit snakes, rivers, and wind.

He writes about men who turn themselves into were-tigers, were-pigs, and were-crocodiles.

There is even a conservation spirit, *hantu songkei*, that undoes snares "to release trapped animals."

One ghost that takes up a large space in the Malaysian/Indonesian psyche is *orang minyak*, "greasy man," who is a slippery take on the Hunchback of Notre Dame. *Orang minyak* wanders around naked, covered in oil, and preys on beautiful young women.

But it is the female ghosts that steal the show.

The *pontianak* is the most prominent of a large sisterhood of feminine spirits who are descended from women who have died in childbirth and who have been abused by men. If you have the patience, gather together some Malay friends and ask them to name and describe the characteristics of the various angry female ghosts. There is considerable overlap and confusion. They are beautiful and entice young men to messy demises. They are old hags with pendulous breasts. Or they exhibit both personas, depending on the situation and who's telling the story.

Here are some of the more well-known forms of female Malay ghosts identified by ghost taxonomists; one could argue that they are variations on a single theme, just as the beagle, the Siberian husky, and the Yorkshire terrier are all the same species: *Canis lupus familiaris.*

* The classic female vampire ghost is called *pontianak* in Malaysia and *kuntilanak* or *matianak* in Indonesia. She is the ghost of a woman who died in childbirth, and sucks blood of virgins and men who have wronged her.

* *Sundel bolong* is the spirit of a woman who has been raped and abandoned to die. She has a deep hollow in her back. Very nasty piece of work.

* *Langsuir* has the ability to fly, like a *pontianak*; she is sometimes associated with the owl, called "ghost bird" in Malay.

* *Hantu tetek*, also known as *hantu kopek*, is a huge old hag with pendulous breasts. Because she preys on children, parents invoke her name to encourage kids to get home in time for *maghrib* (dusk prayer) or risk being captured by *hantu tetek* and smothered to death. Many cultures have this kind of Big Momma Witch – Hansel and Gretel come to mind.

* *Churel* is another female ghost with pendulous breasts, a consistent feature of their kind. And, like other female ghosts, she can also appear as a beautiful young woman who can charm any man. Because young men caused her death during childbirth, the *churel* drinks their blood, beginning with the one she loved in life. There are numerous ways to get rid of a *churel*, including burning a ball of thread along with the body in the belief that the woman's spirit will be so preoccupied with unwinding the ball that she won't bother to haunt anyone.

* *Penanggallan*, which Danny Lim describes as having long flowing hair, penetrating red eyes, and a long protruding tongue. She feeds on human blood and flesh, with a preference for the taste of a newborn infant. When she goes out on the town, she is able to separate her head and organs from the rest of her body; she leaves the rest of her body in a container of vinegar to preserve it until she returns. As Lim says, "A woman smelling of vinegar is not to be trifled with." This head-and-intestines creature seeks houses where women are about to give birth. The way to prevent her entry is by hanging pineapple or pandan thorns around the house; the sharp points will hook the *penanggallan*'s flailing intestinal tracts and entrap the spirit.

"You were so close," Rustammy says. Like a manager talking to a baseball player who hits a long ball that is caught when the outfielder makes a spectacular leaping catch.

But actually I wasn't close at all. I don't believe in this stuff.

"Want to try again?"

Rustammy instructs me to relax, repeat the body posture, and this time he says I should ask the pontianak *to shake my hands.*

I've done this type of thing before. The power of suggestion is a strong power indeed. I hold my hands in front of me, keeping them still. Come on pontianak, *make my hands jiggle.*

I sit there for another few minutes. Nothing. I order the spirit to come to me, to make my hands shake. I command her in English. In Indonesian. In French. In Thai. I run out of languages. Oh yeah, German. That must be a good language for ordering a spirit to come hither. Komm sofort her. *No, make it stronger.* Sonst, *I said with menace in my voice.*

And just for fun I start to wiggle my hand.

And once the wiggling starts, the jiggle and jangle of my hands became stronger and my arms are bouncing around, like a small boat on a rough sea. But I am in control. I could stop it at any moment, but it is sort of fun. Let's see how this plays out.

Come to me. I order you. I humbly request you. Sorry to impose, but I'm only in Pontianak for a short time and it's now or never. I have a story to write.

What a great song Burt Bacharach wrote for Karen and Richard Carpenter.

Karen Carpenter couldn't be a pontianak. *Could she?
No, no way.*

Monkey-mind goes wild. I'm shaking my arms and having a good old time.

Foreplay, but no climax. No ghost appears. After a few more minutes I deliberately stop my flailing arms, take a breath, and open my eyes.

MAYA SATRINI DOESN'T LOOK LIKE A WOMAN WHO could beat up a *pontianak*.

She's a thin, neat, serious grandmother who lives in Singkawang, a small town two hours north of Pontianak.

But Maya has steel in her character.

She runs a non-governmental organization that tries to stop the trafficking in women from the region to men in Hong Kong, Taiwan, and Malaysia. "Young girls from the villages are promised jobs as maids or think they're going to get married," she explained, but often they wind up as "family whores," forced to service many men. They're promised salaries but they receive nothing after the down payment of a few hundred dollars. Eventually they get HIV and are sent back. "Sometimes I get a call in the middle of the night," Maya explains, "to rescue a girl left in the middle of some rural road."

Maya believes the origin of the *pontianak* myth is based on the widespread (and not incorrect) belief that men don't take responsibility for fatherhood.

The first sultan of Pontianak encountered *pontianaks*

when he wanted to make a settlement in the swampy forest. Similarly, Maya's house abuts a forest and she thinks that could be one reason why her son and two grandchildren saw *pontianaks* in front of the family home – it's common knowledge that a wilderness is the haunt of demons.

"*Pontianaks* are spirits that haven't had a chance to settle," she says, explaining that most people die because their contract with Allah is finished. "But some spirits don't go back to Allah immediately; they're waiting for a promise that has yet to be kept."

Several *pontianaks* appeared to Maya a few days before my visit. "It was eight-thirty in the morning," she recalls. "I was in my bedroom. They looked like normal adult women except I could see through them – they were almost transparent."

"One of the ghosts was angry with me," Maya told me. "She knew you were coming and said I mustn't talk with you, that you had no business delving into such things."

Maya said she told the ghost that they had no such agreement. Maya told the spirit to leave.

And then the *pontianak* spit at her.

Maya's face became red and a rash immediately appeared.

And Maya spit back. "The *pontianak's* face became red and her eyes looked like they would burst out of her head," Maya recalled.

The ghosts disappeared. Maya treated her rash, which she described as being "like a bee sting," with an herbal remedy made of charcoal, garlic, onion, and dried chilli. The swelling went away after fifteen minutes.

And then, Dewi, the quiet housewife in the maroon head scarf sitting opposite me, lets out a shriek that, excuse the cliché, could have woken the dead. It is a cinematic screech, worthy of the best (or the worst, it's hard to tell sometimes) pontianak movies. Her voice goes all husky, she lets out a high-pitched "ha-hee-ha-hee" laugh of maleficence that could equally be a cry of anguish.

Her voice can best be described by a phrase I would never allow my writing students to use: blood-curdling. Laughter. Screaming. Crying. Sobbing. "You people are bothering me." Her gaze is distant and unfocused, her eyes hooded, her voice husky. Repeat laughter, screaming, crying, sobbing.

Dewi starts to shake, then jerks around and stands up. Her headscarf goes flying. It looks like she is having an epileptic fit. Softer laugh. "Blood. See the blood!?" she shrieks.

Dewi quiets down a bit. Rustammy speaks to her, asks who she is.

"Farida," she spits out. "My name is Farida. I was killed by a man. I want to go to Meester Paul. He called me."

Meester Paul. That is me.

"I want blood. His blood." Laughter and sobbing.

"I want to return. Don't bother me." Dewi crawls into the next room, her sobbing mixed with a hysterical laugh.

Rustammy calms her down. "Go back. It's okay, Farida. Go back."

Then Dewi erupts again. "I was torn apart. I'll remember his face forever. I don't want to go home. I want to follow Meester."

Dewi collapses. She is lying on her back. She looks like she is in a coma.

Rustammy "wipes" her body to remove the ghost. It's a cleansing action in which he rapidly sweeps the negative energy from Dewi's head, her back, her stomach, her legs. Even Western massage therapists know this move.

After a few minutes Dewi opens her eyes and sits up. We all breathe easier.

AT THE VILLAGE LEVEL, FOLKS LIKE RUSTAMMY "cleanse" the victim. The concept of cleansing has a special place in Indonesia's Islamic community, and Muslim prayers are often invoked.

But is there a deeper intention?

The term "catharsis" is Greek for purging or cleansing. One controversial etymology of the word derives from the Greek *katheiro*, to rid the land of monsters.

Isn't that what a shaman does? He or she helps us banish the demons within. We all tango with our demons, weaving, posturing, conquering and submitting, seducing and sometimes conquering. Demons are our dark sides, our uncontrollable desires, our regrets over actions taken, or not.

WHEREVER THERE ARE GHOSTS THERE ARE SURELY ghostbusters.

A *dukun* has to know not only how to call a spirit, but how to get rid of one.

My friend Amalia is a Singaporean spirit guide who makes a decent living flying around the world cleansing homes and businesses of bad spirits for Beverly Hills-types. I never quite know how serious she is when she tells me about her achievements. You would recognize the names of some of her clients.

VAMPIRE MOVIES SINK THEIR TEETH INTO THEATERS IN most countries. A quick check of the IMDb database gives some two hundred results with "vampire" in the title, including *Jesus Christ Vampire Hunter*, *Vampire Hookers*, *I Bought a Vampire Motorcycle*, and *A Polish Vampire in Burbank*.

Pontianak- and *kuntilanak*-themed films have been box-office favorites in Malaysia and Indonesia since 1958 when the Malaysian film *Anak Pontianak* (Child of Pontianak) was released, followed three years later by the Indonesian film *Kuntilanak*. A spate of female vampire ghost films ensued, followed by a three-decade hiatus. The industry picked up again in the 2000s.

L. Krishnan, one of the pioneers of the Malaysian film industry, is now ninety-three and living in Thailand. His films include some of the classic Malaysian ghost films, such as the 1958 *Serangan Orang Minyak* (Attack of the Orang Minyak).

"No, I don't believe in ghosts, but the people who go to the cinema do," he explained over lunch at a Bangkok café. "There were times when the film was shown in a cinema and the film burned because the projectionist hadn't said the proper prayers."

Shankar Punjabi is another leading horror film director who doesn't believe in ghosts. "No, I've never seen a ghost and I never got possessed. If you believe in ghosts you will see them. It's the power of suggestion, as if I ask you, 'do you feel the wind on your arms?' They go into self-induced trances. Imagination works best in a dark room. If you believe you will feel, if you feel you will see."

Over coffee in a Jakarta restaurant, Indonesia-based Shankar added: "But I've had actors who got haunted, and we always have an *ustadz* [Islamic spiritual teacher] on call during the shoot to treat the crew and actors who get possessed."

Prem Pasha, a Malaysian filmmaker who is L. Krishnan's son, recalled that when he was about seven he visited the set of his father's film that was being shot at night at an old English bungalow in Kuala Lumpur. "I remember that Noordin Ahmad, the star who played the *orang minyak*, approached the camera. I looked up and saw a "real" *orang minyak* watching the proceedings from the balcony where Noordin had just come from."

Teenage boys like to tempt fate, and when Prem was sixteen, he and two friends went to a cemetery to spend the night. He doesn't remember the details, but they were approached by a woman who glowed, like she was covered in diamonds. Prem went into a coma for two days, and when he awoke he was suffering a high fever and his frantic grandmother was rubbing Indian holy ash on his forehead.

I asked if they had called a *bomoh*. "No, ninety-nine point nine percent of *bomohs* are fakes, he said. "But what about spirits and ghosts?" I asked. "Ah. They're real."

Are the *pontianak* films sexist? Glen Goei, who, with Gavin Yap, is writing a new *pontianak* film, thinks they represent the 1950s Malaysian society when men were men and women were women. He didn't say so, and I'm not suggesting he thinks this, but the extension of this idea is that in rural Malay societies women are closer to the spiritual world than men; they have special, often nasty, powers, and are fickle about whom they choose to befriend and whom they elect to curse. Perhaps this is male resentment (or acknowledgment) that Malay women, like women throughout most of Asia, bear the brunt of the labor, take a large chunk of familial responsibility, and are generally the stronger and more reliable of the two genders.

I had coffee with Danny Lim at a Kuala Lumpur café. Lim, who wrote the *Malaysian Book of the Undead*, agrees that ghost stories and films reflect rural, village life. "You don't have many urban ghosts," he says, although some modern ghost films feature sophisticated urban men (usually spoiled playboys and businessmen) encountering traditional spirits.

The Indonesian film industry is in the doldrums, and according to film journalist Bobby Batara, it's due to poor governance. There are about one hundred and twenty Indonesian films made each year, Bobby says, of which about twenty are horror films. "The government regulation of 2009 specifies that there should be two Indonesian films distributed nationally for each foreign film, but the handful of cinema owners who control the market ignore that ruling. Indonesian filmmakers have to beg, bribe, and coerce to get their films shown."

I WANTED TO SPEAK WITH AN ACTRESS WHO PLAYED A vampire ghost. I was introduced to Julia Perez by a mutual friend, a leading Indonesian film producer. I was in Jakarta, and she was in a Singapore hospital. I was surprised she bothered to exchange SMS messages with me to set up a phone interview; the day before our talk she had undergone an operation for cervical cancer.

Known by her nickname Jupe (pronounced Joo-Pay), her career has risen due largely to her energetic portrayal of sexy and nasty ghosts. She has starred in some of the most famous Indonesian *kuntilanak* films such as *Jeritan Kuntilanak* (Scream of the Kuntilanak), *Kuntilanak Kesurupan* (Trance of the Kuntilanak), *Kuntilanak Kamar Mayat* (The Mortuary Ghost), and *Beranak Dalam Kubur* (Birth in the Graveyard).

"Acting in a horror movie is not difficult," Jupe says. "They're the same as any action movie."

But has she seen ghosts while making her films?

"Not clearly, not in front of my face, but I've seen strange shadows. My grandmother told me they exist."

I didn't know how hard to push a woman who had just had major surgery, but I asked whether she believed in these spirits.

"I believe fifty percent. There are mystical things we have to respect. But the other fifty percent is just human behavior." It was a similar answer to the question I had been posing so frequently – maybe, who knows, I'm not sure, I saw something I can't explain, better not examine it too closely.

FOLLOWING IS A BIT OF HOOPTEDOODLE (SEE JOHN Steinbeck).

Julia Perez is one of Indonesia's most hardworking actresses; her career has blossomed partly because of her outspoken approach to life and performing.

Jupe has written a book in which she describes the secret of her success: The Five Bs: beauty, brains, behave, bitchy, and boobs. This is not the place to elaborate on her life strategy, but no doubt a Ph.D. awaits someone who can put a post-modern Indonesian spin on her philosophy.

In August 2012 Jupe carried out a promise that when she reached one million Twitter followers she would perform a pole dance at a busy traffic intersection in downtown Jakarta. This performance, plus the fact that she wore skimpy clothing, plus the fact that it was the

Muslim fasting month, did not endear her to the more conservative of Jakarta's tastemakers.

Moralistic officials and religious leaders abhor her sexy persona and denounce her suggestive singing and dancing (she is probably responsible for the creation of the Indonesian word *bomseks*, from the English "sex bomb"). Righteous men and women have banned her from performing in many cities. Jupe defends herself by asking, and I'm paraphrasing: *The men who criticize me are the ones who take bribes, who cheat on their wives, who use taxpayer money to line their own bank accounts. Who is committing the sin? Me, who entertains people or these hypocritical men, who steal from the people?*

Meanwhile, a few meters away, Rustammy's wife Anni, who had been drinking tea and chatting with friends, becomes possessed. She doesn't shout, but her eyes roll up in their sockets and she is quietly sick. The spirits are up and about, targeting impressible women.

Just as Westerners are taught the Heimlich maneuver, most Indonesians seem to know how to ask a spirit to leave. Someone puts his hand on Anni's forehead, and "sweeps" away the spirit, while mumbling some Islamic prayers. Anni is an elegant woman, wearing a dress with a Burberry-style plaid. She calms down, a bit embarrassed by the mess she has made.

HOW CAN YOU RECOGNIZE A *PONTIANAK*? AND, MORE importantly, what can you do when confronted by one?

Her presence can sometimes be detected by a sweet floral fragrance identifiable as that of the plumeria, followed by an awful stench afterward.

A *pontianak* kills her victims by digging into their stomachs with her sharp fingernails and devouring their organs. In some cases where the *pontianak* desires revenge against a man, she rips out the guy's sex organs with her hands. It is said that if you have your eyes open when a *pontianak* is near, she will suck them out of your head. *Pontianaks* locate prey by sniffing out clothes left outside to dry. For this reason, some people refuse to leave any article of clothing outside of their residences overnight.

And most insidious, the *pontianak* announces her presence through baby cries. If the cry is loud then the ghost must be far away. If the baby's cry is soft, then she is close, ready to punish a man. It doesn't really matter to the *pontianak* whether the man she has targeted is good or evil; all men are same-same, which is to say all men, according to her definition, deserve to die.

I kneel down next to Dewi and ask if she has any recollection of what had just happened. And she goes wild. It is a false calm. Farida has not left at all but was lying in wait, like a hibernating bear. Dewi screams and sobs and laughs. This time she looks straight at me. "I want to follow you. You follow me to the cemetery."

She picks up a plastic water bottle and throws it across the room.

Dewi holds out her hand, wants me to take it so she can guide me to the cemetery. I refuse. Her eyes bulge, unfocused. "Meester," she says, using the expression Indonesians in an earlier generation used to address Dutchmen. "Meester. You called me. I am Farida. You wanted to see me. I am here for you."

WHY DO GHOST STORIES LINGER IN SO MANY countries?

Some people feel the *pontianak* is an enforcer of morality, a creation of Malay wives who wanted to discourage their husbands from engaging in casual sex with women they might meet on the road at night. Be faithful, the man is told, and he won't have any supernatural complications.

Dimas Jayasrana is an Indonesian film producer who thinks that an encounter with a ghost is like meeting a superstar. "Seeing an old lady in a white dress who is dripping blood and laughing like a little girl is the village equivalent of running into George Clooney." And, Dimas adds, ghosts are useful for disciplining kids. All cultures have tales of ogre-like beings. In the English-speaking world we are told "be good or the bogeyman will get you." The bogeyman, so feared by young children, is a linguistic creation inspired by the Bugis, a race of Indonesian seafarers (and sometimes pirates) for whom the British colonials developed a healthy fear.

Dewi crawls into the next room, knocks over a table with coffee cups, and then crashes into a computer printer. She huddles in a corner, then squats on a chair.

I don't get too close to her. But she approaches me. "Meeesterrrr," she says, rolling her Rs in a supernatural vibrato, drawing out the two-syllable word for several seconds. "Meee-Sterrr. You called me. Fifteen years. I am Farida. You called me."

Fifteen years? I have no idea if that was her age when she died, or how long she's been in this place between two worlds.

Dewi then ignores me, like a small child who's bored with a toy. She shudders and Rustammy goes to her to cleanse her once again.

THE *PONTIANAK* IS AN EQUAL-OPPORTUNITY GHOST. IN multicultural Malaysia, where Malays, Chinese, and Indians live side by side but not always tension-free, *pontianaks* traverse racial, religious and urban/rural differences.

Pontianaks have, so far, escaped the scrutiny of the Islamic fundamentalists in Malaysia. These are the fun-killing folks who have outlawed Halloween because it's both too Christian and too pagan. This dress-up holiday is "associated with the devil" and is "clearly contrary to the values of Sharia," according to the National Fatwa Council, Malaysia's top Islamic body.

Perhaps because *pontianaks* are home-grown they are culturally acceptable. As Amir Muhammad writes in the forward to *The Malaysian Book of the Undead*, "The ghosts we choose to believe in can also say a lot about our attitudes towards gender, the natural environment and even race."

Rustammy brings Dewi out of the trance, and this time it seems like Farida has genuinely left.

"So, you saw a pontianak," *Rustammy says to me.*

"But she didn't come when I called her myself," I say.

"But that's exactly what did happen. You called her and she came to you, through Dewi. You saw Farida. She'll be with you tonight."

I think about that for a moment and say. "Never mind, that's okay. I got what I came for."

And Rustammy gets really pissed off. "But you called her. She came. You have a deal."

My monkey-mind recalls the story "The Devil and Daniel Webster." Faust and all that. I don't have a valid contract with a pontianak. *Or do I?*

Of course I don't believe all this stuff. But I also don't want to insult my hosts by appearing to not take it seriously. "What can we do?"

Rustammy is obviously disappointed in my lack of commitment. "You're not convinced, I can see that. But still, you called her, and she came."

And so?

"Chicken blood should do the trick."

I look bewildered. Rustammy explains:"She wants your blood. But she'll settle for chicken blood."

It is about midnight on a Sunday night. We are in a middle-class, residential neighborhood of Pontianak. You can't just go into the backyard and grab a chicken. And the live chicken market is surely closed.

But this is Indonesia, and everything is possible. I dig into my wallet and hand a few bills to a young man. Forty-five minutes later he comes back with an unhappy-looking red chicken strapped to his motorcycle handlebars.

"Do I need to kill it myself?" I ask.

"No, since you're not a true believer we can do it. You can go home."

I don't like the religious connotation of whether I am a "believer," but perhaps I am overreacting.

To be certain I ask one last time.

"So this will satisfy Farida and keep her happy?"

"It should be okay. She probably won't bother you tonight," Rustammy says. "But you never know."

IT'S NOT HARD TO SEE HOW THE GUIDED TRANCE STATE of a *pontianak* séance uses similar dynamics to some religions and cults. "Do you believe?" Do you *really* believe? Do you want the Holy Spirit to enter you and save you? Like Molly Bloom you spurt out "Yes! Yes! Yes!" Then comes speaking in tongues, fainting, signing over the deed to your house and dancing with rattle-snakes. A true believer is born.

I return to my comfortable hotel around one in the morning, have a shower, and hop into bed. I have no fear that a pontianak *has followed me home. I don't believe in such stuff. I turn the air-con up and snuggle in for a good rest.*

Just as I am hitting that never-never land between consciousness and sleep, I hear a faint sound that jars me awake. I listen more carefully. It is the cry of a baby. Unmistakable. Coming from the next room. Damn, that meddling pontianak *Farida did follow me home.*

And then I remember. Earlier in the day I had heard a baby crying in the adjoining room. Parents traveling with a young child; so common in Indonesia as not to be worth a second thought. Surely that is the baby's cry I hear. Of course it isn't a pontianak. *Surely not. Just a normal human baby crying for a feed. Isn't it?*

ABOUT THE AUTHOR

Paul, reading Alfred Russel Wallace, in a
tributary of the Batang Ai, Sarawak.
Photo: William J. Stone

PAUL SPENCER SOCHACZEWSKI has written *Share Your Journey, An Inordinate Fondness for Beetles, The Sultan and the Mermaid Queen, Redheads, Soul of the Tiger* (co-authored with Jeff McNeely), and other acclaimed books, along with some six hundred bylined articles in leading international publications. He has lived and worked in more than eighty countries, including long stints in Southeast Asia.

Visit Paul at:
www.sochaczewski.com

www.ingramcontent.com/pod-product-compliance
Lightning Source LLC
Chambersburg PA
CBHW020241130626
46549CB00005B/2010